Recreating the Workplace

Oliver Wight Publications, Inc.

EXECUTIVE BREAKTHROUGH SERIES

First Launch: Leveraging the Power of
Integrated Product Development
by V. Daniel Hunt (Avail. October 1993)

Recreating the Workplace: The Pathway
to High Performance Work Systems
by Steven R. Rayner (Avail. June 1993)

Breakthrough Partnering: Creating a
Collective Enterprise Advantage
by Patricia E. Moody (Avail. October 1993)

Planning & Control in the Age of Lean Production
by Darryl V. Landvater (Avail. January 1994)

Quantum Leap: Achieving Strategic
Breakthroughs with QFD
by Thomas F. Wallace and William Barnard
(Avail. November 1993)

In the Age of the Real-Time Enterprise
by Tom Gunn (Avail. November 1993)

Recreating the Workplace

THE PATHWAY TO HIGH PERFORMANCE WORK SYSTEMS

Steven R. Rayner

THE OLIVER WIGHT COMPANIES

Oliver Wight Publications, Inc.
5 Oliver Wight Drive
Essex Junction, VT 05452

For Colleen

Acknowledgments

There are many who have contributed—either directly or indirectly—to the completion of this book. Their ideas and insights, support and encouragement were invaluable. To them I owe much thanks and gratitude.

In 1989 Bill Belgard, Kim Fisher, and I founded Belgard•Fisher•Rayner, Inc. (BFR). Much of what we have tried to create for our clients and within BFR itself is reflected on the pages in this book. We have not always succeeded, but I think it is fair to say we have always "dared greatly."

To Bill and Kim I owe a much personal thanks. Many of their experiences and observations are contained throughout this work, but far more important has been their support as partners, colleagues, and friends. Having had the opportunity to work closely with Bill and Kim for nearly a decade has been the highlight of my professional career. I am sure the coming decade will be equally as rewarding.

My other coworkers at BFR made this book possible by taking on additional work while I was busily writing and editing. In this sense the book was truly a team effort. Without their willingness to believe in and support me, the book would've been little more than a distant dream.

The process for implementing high performance teams described in Chapter 3 began as an after-work conversation topic a number of years ago with two colleagues, Jim Armstrong and Mike Hunter. We regularly met at a local pizza parlor, where we became engaged in long discussions about how to most effectively implement and sustain culture change within an organization. The process we originally defined during these colorful discussions has been modified and improved over the years, but the foundation the original thinking provided has clearly stood the test of time.

In conducting research, I was fortunate to have the talented and highly disciplined support of Merle Hellickson. His inquisitive mind left few stones unturned as he piled through countless articles and books and conducted a number of interviews. Merle's commitment to the project was an inspiration.

There are numerous cases and examples mentioned in the book, but I would like to single out the following individuals for letting me re-tell their remarkable stories: Joe Burger, Allen Class, Fred Hanson, Ed Kilroy, Bob Horton, John Adamoli, Brian Reynolds, Ralph Olney, and Don Bell. I also learned a great deal about organization change and team implementation through several interviews with some truly "leading edge" managers. They contributed many ideas that proved invaluable. Thanks to Carl Martin, Ray Thompson, Mike Bleck, Rex Perkes, Keith Sletter, Len Hall, Don Lyon, Dan Snell, Paul O'Bierne, Brad Baker, and, finally, Mike Murray, whose personal motto—"Empower every employee to make a positive contribution every workday"—says a lot about his management style.

My parents, George and Ruby Rayner, helped me out as well. My father, now retired, related the many things he had learned in his twenty-plus years of management. He, I might add, had been a management innovator in his own right. He was experimenting with self-directed work teams well over a decade ago. My mother, figuring I could always use a little extra help with the research, started cutting out articles she thought I might find useful. Many of the articles turned out to be of great interest and prompted ideas that I incorporated into the text.

Jim Childs, my editor, deserves much credit for the book's readability. From the beginning, Jim and I developed a strong working relationship. I eagerly looked forward to hearing his critiques and quickly incorporated his many insightful suggestions. Jim also had a knack for giving me encouragement when I needed it most.

My wife, Colleen Keefe, to whom this book is dedicated, contributed in innumerable ways. She provided ideas based on her own management experience, took on double parenting duties with our twin sons during the months of writing and editing which consumed both my weekdays and weekends, and always conveyed her belief in me and what I hoped to accomplish with the book. During the days when the writing wasn't going well, her wit—which is truly second to none—would always put my frustrations at ease.

Steven R. Rayner
Freeland, Washington
February 1993

Contents

List of Figures

Introduction

Upon graduating from college, I had an inside track on a job at a local high-tech firm. The job posting said the firm was looking for a "project historian." Not fully understanding why a company would want a historian, or what the position would require me to do, I went to the interview and gave it my best shot. A week or so later I received a job offer. Little did I know then just how much studying the past was about to prepare me for the future.

For the next eighteen months I conducted hundreds of interviews, reviewed thousands of documents, and began writing about one of the most innovative management experiments going on anywhere in the country. The plant manager explained that I had been hired as a kind of communication tool. It was his hope that my account of how the plant operated would help spread interest in its management approach to other divisions within the company and to other companies across the industry. "What we're doing here is going to change U.S. manufacturing," he'd boast.

The four-hundred-person plant was, indeed, remarkable. It was organized into fourteen manufacturing teams and five support groups, had just two levels of management, and relied on direct employee participation in deciding everything from what color to paint the cafeteria to what business strategies to pursue. Employee participation was such a core fixture of the work culture that even the compensation system—which the employees themselves had designed—was linked to a combination of individual contribution to the team, job skills, business knowledge, and plant performance.

THE COMMITMENT FACTOR

While there were countless features about the plant that made it unique—from its having no quality inspection, to its monthly assemblies where the entire membership of the facility met for an hour, to its garden area where employees planted and harvested vegetables for their personal consumption—it was the commitment of the people working at the site that left the strongest impression on me. In one case, several employees brought in sleeping bags so they could correct a process problem during the evening rather than "waste" part of the next day's production time. The manager of the area was shocked the following morning when he learned that the weary-eyed operators had spent the entire night working on the nagging problem. This example typified the way the majority of employees at the facility felt and operated—they were profoundly committed.

Management clearly played an important role in fostering the commitment. "Our objective is to develop the capabilities of our people," noted the plant manager. "Our business performance will be a reflection of how well we do it." The words were backed up with extensive training and development that, in addition to classroom sessions, included rotations, cross-training, advanced degrees—even study abroad.

A FORESHADOWING OF THINGS TO COME

I was deeply affected by the experience—especially when I began to recognize just how unique this plant's management system was in relation to the way most U.S. and Canadian firms operated. At the center of focus was the customer. Those actually performing the work were provided with the necessary information, tools, training, and decision-making authority to assure that the customer's needs were met. Managers played an equally active and equally nontraditional role. They focused on such things as developing the capabilities of the team, breaking down barriers, examining new technologies, studying competitor products and processes, and working closely with customers and vendors. The bottom line of it all was impressive—30 percent better than comparable plants in virtually every measure (i.e., output, quality, delivery, throughput, sales per employee).

The plant's team-based system was a foreshadowing of the direction that management practices across North America were headed. In the early Eighties, one rarely encountered terms like "self-directed work teams," "self-management," or "employee empowerment." But by the Nineties, it had become nearly impossible to find a company that didn't have some effort under way to increase the involvement of its employees. Today it is commonly accepted that the premier organizations of tomorrow will be the ones that most effectively unleash the creative potential of their work force.

THE SHIFTING SANDS OF CHANGE

Since my tenure as project historian, over a decade ago now, I have had the opportunity to work with a number of managers who are grappling with the same question: How do I transform my organization into a high performing work system? Ironically, while there is considerable recognition that the workplace of tomorrow will be team-based, highly responsive to market demands and opportunities, able to pool together talent quickly, and continually developing and enhancing the capabilities of its only appreciable asset—its employees—there are no standard models, processes, or recipes for how to implement a high performance work system. Unfortunately, many take the easy road, bringing in the newest fad or program with the sincere hope that a quick and easy fix is possible.

Programs ultimately fail because they do not attempt to change the *core* of the organization. Its fundamental systems, processes, and structures—its very culture—are left unaltered. Change happens at a cosmetic level, creating the outward—and often temporary—appearance of change, while the inner core continues to operate as it always has.

I have observed and experienced the many frustrations associated with program failures. I have even been party to such efforts—caught up in the belief that there really was a quick and easy fix. Creating a true high performance work system requires going far beyond programmatic change. It is neither easy nor quick. It requires a proven process that focuses on changing the cultural fabric of the organization.

BEYOND COSMETIC CHANGE

For the manager who wishes to go beyond cosmetic change, looking upward at the layers of hierarchy and across at the multitude of functional departments, the task of creating a high performing work system looks daunting. Questions abound:

- Where does one begin?
- What is the best pathway to follow?
- How important is it to have senior-management support?
- From what group will the greatest amount of resistance emerge?
- What happens to middle managers?
- When should changes to the compensation system occur?
- What are the "essentials" that must be in place to assure that the transition will be successful?

- What's the most effective way to increase the flow of information so that it reinforces team development?
- What type of team structure should be used?
- Why does the level of performance improvement among some teams begin to flatten over time? What can be done about it?

This book was written with these questions in mind. It provides:

1. A proven and comprehensive process for making the transition to a high performance work system
2. Specific strategies for addressing the many complex issues implementers are likely to face

The demands placed on the modern manager are indeed intense. The work group he manages or the organization she leads must become more efficient, flexible, responsive, customer-oriented, and innovative. The structures, systems, and processes of yesteryear are simply too antiquated to meet these demands. The future requires nothing less than recreating the workplace.

PART ONE

The Teaming Advantage

*P*rofound and powerful forces are shaking and remaking our world, and the urgent question of our age is whether we can make change our friend and not our enemy.

From President Bill Clinton's
Inauguration Address, 1993

CHAPTER 1

The Age of
Teaming

Large-scale bureaucracy is so wrought with inefficiency that modern demands have made it an untenable form of organization. The few remaining Neanderthal organizations will either re-create themselves or become history's next victims. The current large-scale movement among corporate leaders to break away from their bureaucratic past and adopt a team-based design is not a temporary phenomenon. It is here to stay, and it is an issue of survival.

The gains documented in many team-based organizations have been startling—in the 20 to 40 percent range in productivity and quality measures. Equally impressive are reports of dramatic cost savings (20 to 30 percent range), reduced time to market (50 to 60 percent), safety improvements (15 to 20 percent), and improved quality of work life (15 to 40 percent). Stories like these abound:

- After introducing the team approach, a processing group at Eastman Kodak saw performance improvement in every category they measure.

- An engineering team at Tektronix cut its time to market for new-product introductions from five years to eighteen months.
- The use of work teams has enabled Levi Strauss to reduce the time needed to produce a garment—from material delivery to shipment of jeans—from five days to one.[1]
- Steelcase estimates that employee ideas save the company more than $1.2 million annually.[2]

Examples of significant improvement are easy to find in virtually every industry sector across North America and western Europe. Managers are quickly realizing that ignoring the potential of team-based work systems could well be disastrous. As Northern Telecom plant manager Debra Boggan explains:

> In the 1990s, successful companies will . . . put innovation back in the workplace. As plant manager, I felt much more comfortable knowing that 420 people were worried about my business, rather than just my senior management team of 15. . . . Empowering employees—giving them responsibility for the business—is the key.[3]

THE WORK TEAM LINKAGE

Whether one is talking about Total Quality Management (TQM), Just-in-Time manufacturing (JIT), Materials Requirements Planning (MRP), or service excellence, employee involvement plays a critical role in its success. Quality guru W. Edwards Deming's fourteen points for building a quality culture focus almost entirely on issues relating to empowerment. Similarly, the TQM objectives specified by the government for its contractors and much of the criteria associated with the Malcolm Baldrige Award emphasize the importance of highly participative work systems. Any organization that is considering improving its product quality, productivity, ability to innovate, service, or employee relations has to seriously consider these innovative work systems.

Today, virtually every major corporation is experimenting with team-based work design—up from a tiny percentage of companies that did so a decade ago. It is staggering to consider that by the turn of the century half of all employees will find themselves operating as members of a team. This widespread change in management philosophy has profound implications—it suggests changes in the assumptions, practices, culture, structures, and processes all across corporate America. Entire corporations will be designed as team-based work systems. Others, failing to embrace the new design, will fall behind their more productive and nimble competitors. The complexion of business will be changed forever as a workplace revolution, unprecedented in scope since the beginning of industrialization, sweeps across the country.

THE AGE OF TEAMING

Effectively implementing high performing teams is emerging as a central organizational concern for most companies. The 1990s will likely be remembered as the "Age of Teaming" as corporations audaciously attempt to re-create the workplace. Undoubtedly, some will succeed with fabulous results while others—perhaps even the majority—will adopt the team banner and learn the vocabulary while experiencing little substantive change.

Much of the pervasive wisdom on how to design and manage large companies runs counter to the concepts behind team-based work systems. Consider the emphasis on departmentalization, narrowly defined jobs, specialists, rigid hierarchy, and "need to know" information passing—all factors dominant in most organizations and that are damning to a team-based approach. Many of the fundamental assumptions widely held about the very practice of management and organization design are direct relics of the early 1900s. The barriers to change that this long-standing tradition creates are substantial. Estimates vary, but somewhere between 40 and 60 percent of all current attempts to create team-based work cultures results in no performance improvement. The dark forces of tradition are prevalent, while the need for corporate transformation is greater than ever before.

DESTINATION MEDIOCRITY

While a growing number of companies are experimenting with teams, these experiments are still happening on a relatively small scale—often among just a few work teams representing a fraction of the company's total population. No major corporation has yet introduced teams across the board, nor are any currently contemplating doing so. This is due, in part, to the roller-coaster results often seen between various teams within the same company. This performance inconsistency heightens management reluctance to pursue teaming across a wide segment of the organization. In Martin Marietta's Astronautics Group, for example, the wire harness team and the boat-tail assembly area demonstrated spectacular improvements in eliminating redundant work processes and shortening overall production time after a team-based system was implemented. In sharp contrast, a neighboring manufacturing area showed no significant improvement. After several months of mediocre performance, the neighboring area's management introduced a new program called the "focus factory." According to a senior manager, the reason for the change was that "we have moved our organization beyond teams—we no longer need them." Others saw it as a way to mask their failure to produce any tangible results.

Hopping on the band wagon to implement teams may result in little more than a ride to Destination Mediocrity. In many organizations "teams" are little more than the next "program du jour." Managers, sincere in their desire to improve their organization's performance, quickly adopt the latest fad with little understanding of the profound implications. Consultants, sometimes more focused on getting a good contract than on what is truly in their client's best interest, too often perpetuate the belief in the possibility of a quick and easy fix. The result is lots of activity, but few results. As one aggravated employee summarized his experience with Rockwell's various programs and initiatives, "We've tried it all and done absolutely none of it."

THE ORGANIZATION AS AN ECOSYSTEM

For years environmentalists have been stressing the importance of looking at the planet as a whole, integrated ecosystem. Depletion of the ozone, the increase of industrial pollutants, and the devastation of the great rain forests all have far-reaching, global consequences. In many respects the same is true of an organization—it consists of a number of elements that together form a single, integrated system. If we are trying to improve organization performance, it is critical that we attempt to improve the entire system, not just a piece of it like a department or functional group. Curbing deforestation will have little positive effect on global warming if the levels of automobile emissions and industrial pollutants continue to rise. Likewise, "implementing" teams will have little positive impact on organization performance if there is poor leadership support or if there are no changes to the authority/responsibility structure, allowing team members the opportunity to develop and implement their ideas for improvement. This is the problem with programmatic change: It focuses on a piece of the system, and not the whole.

Addressing the organization as a whole, integrated system is critical to successful long-term change. Many efforts at change fail simply because this perspective is never considered. Providing employees extensive training in various quality-improvement techniques does little good if employees aren't allowed any meeting time to discuss quality issues. Introducing skill-based pay will do nothing to promote the acquisition of new skills if there is inadequate time devoted to cross training. A manager at Tektronix simply said "Forget it" when confronted with the amount of information he needed to convey to his work group. "We're doing fine the way things are now." To his credit he didn't raise any false expectations among group members that were later dashed. He recognized some of the direct implications of a team organization and decided it was too much of a stretch for the payback he anticipated.

ROLLER-COASTER RESULTS

Often the reaction is different. Expectations are sometimes raised to enormous heights that cannot possibly be met. This was part of the problem that arose at Martin Marietta and helps explain the roller-coaster results they experienced with high performance work teams (HPWT). Each manufacturing employee went through two days of introductory training at Denver's Scanticon Hotel. During the session they learned what a HPWT was, how roles would need to change to be effective, and how to develop charters for their work teams. The session closed with a question-and-answer period with senior managers—the first time there had ever been this type of open, frank dialogue between management and hourly workers. As one employee reported, raising his right hand above his head, "The expectations at Scanticon were up here, but what we could realistically change was still down here," and he lowered his left hand below his knees. "It was a drag when we got back to work and realized just how far we had to go."

The teams that later proved so successful—the total cost savings Martin Marietta claimed following its first eighteen months with HPWTs was well over $10 million—tended to have the most support from management, were given the most time to develop, saw information passing increase, and were directly involved in work design decisions. In the areas where the effort failed to produce significant results, little changed in the way the immediate organization operated following the training. Systems, processes, and structures remained unaltered. The whole training experience was seen as little more than senior management's latest fad—just another program.

When managers see a new program that receives little support, a debilitating cycle begins. One failed program often leads to another. Ultimately, line managers became cynical about these efforts, showing less and less commitment and support each time the cycle repeats itself.

WHAT IS A HIGH PERFORMANCE WORK SYSTEM?

Surprisingly, many who are in the midst of implementing the "team concept" wouldn't be able to provide a satisfactory answer to this question. Confusion abounds—largely the result of a nearly endless litany of terms commonly used both in the literature and within organizations. The following is just a sample of some common terms used to describe teams:

- Socio-technical system
- High commitment system
- Technician system
- High involvement
- Employee involvement
- People involvement
- Participative management
- Self-management
- Bossless system
- Self-directed work teams
- Empowered work teams
- High performance work system

Are there useful distinctions here? Is a self-directed work team, for example, different from an organization that is using high involvement? The answer is both yes and no—depending on your company. At Goodyear "self-directed work team" describes a group that operates without any direct supervision—like the teams in place at their Mt. Pleasant, Iowa, facility. The distinction within other companies is typically less clear. What's called a self-directed work team in one division may be a quality circle in another. High involvement sometimes means employees get more information than they did under the old management system—but little more. Some managers use vocabulary as a way to create the perception of change when, in fact, the organization is essentially unaltered. Other organizations, like Tektronix in the 1980s, used a variety of terms—people involvement, technician system, socio-tech—that were all interchangeable. "What's important," a senior manager emphasized, "is not the name but that we adhere to a common philosophy of increased participation and involvement as a means to improve business performance."

There are many definitions proposed by various academics, consultants, and managers to try and capture the essence of empowered organizations. Most tend to focus on issues like the amount of information available, the degree of knowledge required, the way power is shared, and the manner in which rewards are allocated. Others emphasize the physical structure of the organization, such as the number of management levels or the manner in which teams are utilized. Throughout this book I will use a single term—high performance work system, or HPWS—to convey a precise meaning. It will denote organizations that achieve extraordinary results through their effective utilization of six core characteristics.

1. Leadership That Empowers Others

Large-scale organization change inevitably means trauma. During the change effort the charter of many departments and groups will be significantly altered or the groups may disband entirely; some individuals will see their status, power, and position threatened while others will be confused and frustrated as new roles and expectations are thrust upon them. If change were easy, it seems only logical that the largest companies of the 1980s—the ones with dominance in their respective industries—would be the dominant companies of the Nineties, yet fully one-third of the Fortune 500 in 1980 are not on the same list today. As with the tyrannosaurus, great size and strength ultimately became a disadvantage when faced with a hostile climate.

What does this have to do with defining a HPWS? Simple: Organization change rarely happens without the emergence of a leader(s) who, through his intense convictions, serves as the sponsor, supporter, and even cheerleader for the effort. There are far too many forces maintaining the status quo for it to be disrupted without a *champion for change* who has a legitimate level of power and influence. HPWS do not suddenly happen—at their genesis are people of conviction.

This is equally true in sustaining the HPWS through time. Leaders like Ralph Olney, the head of Kodak's 13 Room, and Gene Hendrickson, plant manager of Tektronix's circuit board manufacturing facility, continue to play key roles in their respective organizations. And the modeling they set forth is now being exemplified by a new generation of leaders they helped develop. HPWSs are leadership intensive.

2. A Relentless Focus on Strategy and Results

Going to a team-based structure will accomplish little if the change is not concretely tied to an organization's overall strategic direction. In fact, HPWSs must be thought of as means to an end and not an end in themselves. Take the human-relations movement as an example to illustrate this point. In the 1960s the best minds in the organization development field were advocating that managers "get in touch" with their feelings and improve their interpersonal skills as a way to lead their respective companies to improved performance. The "make everybody happy workplace," as cynics called it, had limited success not because the ideas weren't good but, rather, because there was no clear connection between the encounter group meetings that managers suddenly found themselves attending and overall organization strategy. What did getting in touch with personal feelings have to do with lowering manufacturing cost or improving service quality? they wondered.

Managers must be very clear about the strategy they are pursuing and the results they hope to achieve to improve the performance of their business, whether those are lower costs, faster time to market, or improved customer service. Once these goals are clear—very clear—then discussion can begin on how teams may (or may not) help the organization facilitate the execution of the strategy and the attainment of the desired results.

In high performing work systems the connection between business strategy, team structure, work design, and individual roles must be obvious.

3. Open Sharing of Relevant Information

Historically, the flow of information followed a linear path upward to the privileged few. Those managers and directors lucky enough to see the figures, graphs, and charts were told by their superiors that such information was confidential. Breakdowns of financial information, like profit and loss statements, were almost never presented to or distributed among "lower-echelon" workers. Employees typically found out about the performance of their company through the *Wall Street Journal* or the annual report.

Among HPWSs information flows like water, seeping its way into every nook and cranny in the organization. Teams absorb this information and utilize it to help in problem solving, developing innovations, and making decisions. The "need to know" information practices of the past are eclipsed as virtually all relevant business information is openly shared with virtually everyone. People are, in effect, treated like business partners who—with their vested interest in the superior performance of the company—receive the information they need in order to make positive contributions.

4. Borderless Sharing of Power

Authority, responsibility, and power are openly shared between teams and among team members in HPWSs. Authority and power no longer reside within different levels of the hierarchy—it is shared based on the issue being addressed, not based on one's position or status. The clear guideline is that those most directly affected by an issue, problem, or strategy will be involved in addressing it.

Management maintains primary responsibility for setting boundary conditions—the parameters the team must work within because of budgetary, legal, timing, or strategic requirements. Well-developed boundaries provide the team focus and increased autonomy while protecting the organization against unforeseen blunders. Over time, as the team increases in sophistication and experience, its boundaries increase in scope, assuring the team ever-increasing autonomy.

5. A Team-Based Design

The overall organization design reflects an emphasis on teams as the primary work unit. Team membership is sometimes permanent, sometimes temporary, and sometimes a combination of both depending on such things as the team's defined charter, its need for highly specialized expertise, and the nature of the problem, project, or issue it is attempting to address. The team is responsible for the design of its work, including determining required technology and individual work roles.

6. Teamwork Reinforced Through Rewards

Both formal and informal rewards reinforce the overall team-based design. There is a clear linkage between improvements made by the team and the rewards team members receive (e.g., profit sharing, gain sharing, etc.). A variety of methods are used to gain performance feedback at both the team and individual levels, including customer, peer, and management feedback.

ORGANIZATIONAL REVOLUTION

These six characteristics help us clearly distinguish between a HPWS and other forms of employee participation. Suggestion box programs or quality circles, for example, fall short in virtually every characteristic: They generally require little leadership commitment, are typically implemented without any linkage to business strategy, require no substantive change in the way information flows, do not rely on any shift in the balance of authority and power, may actually create dynamics that are counter to teams, and, finally, do little to reinforce the team-based design and to reward team participation. High performance work systems represent such a fundamental shift in the way organizations are designed and operate that Allied-Signal CEO Lawrence Bossidy calls them an "organizational revolution."[4]

It is no surprise that the organizations that have experienced the biggest gains from employee empowerment are the same ones that have most fully developed these six core characteristics. Several software labs at IBM Canada have made dramatic strides over the last two years in developing these traits. Their teams are operating with unprecedented levels of autonomy—more like miniature businesses than a functional technology group. Quality and output have increased as have other, less tangible but equally important elements like creativity and responsiveness. "We have clearly proven it works," noted one software engineer, "but how do we spread it to the rest of the organization?"

THE THREE DILEMMAS

The dilemma IBM faces, as do many other companies that have experimented with HPWSs, is how to take a good idea and see it successfully transferred to other parts of the organization. As William Buehler, senior vice president of Xerox, notes, "You can see a high performance factory or office, but it just doesn't spread."[5] The sheer logic of using teams and the often dramatic results they produce account for remarkably little in the eyes of neighboring organizations. The "not invented here" syndrome—the tendency to discount the successes of other groups as not being relevant to your own organization—is so pervasive that it is arguably the reason such progressive firms as Procter & Gamble and Kodak have had such limited success in transferring HPWSs to larger segments of the company. This is the first dilemma of implementation: the size or coverage of the effort.

The second dilemma managers face relates to the speed of the change. Any in-depth review of the literature substantiates the worst fears of most managers—HPWSs require a long-term transition that rarely yields immediate results. "Everything I read says this is a three-to-five-year transition. I need to see it working next Monday!" cried one frustrated manager. The speed of implementation is increasingly becoming an issue—and the three-to-seven-year time period the literature describes is simply too long. Most companies that are seriously pursuing HPWSs do not have years to develop and cultivate their teams. Rather, they have months and they need to see immediate performance improvements.

The third implementation dilemma centers around sustaining the HPWS through time. Many highly successful HPWSs simply do not endure. Digital's Enfield, Connecticut, plant is a striking example of an organization that demonstrated superior results for more than a decade before it was shut down during a consolidation effort. Following the turnaround at Tektronix's Portable Oscilloscope Division, where HPWSs were widely acknowledged as the key ingredient for its success—a turnaround that was far more dramatic than the highly publicized one at Harley-Davidson—senior-management changes at Tektronix left HPWSs all but abandoned. To have gone through the difficulty of introducing a new management system only to see it erode and dissipate is devastating to both individuals and the organization as a whole.

In all, these form the three implementation dilemmas: size, speed, and sustainability. The three dilemmas can best be stated as questions:

1. How can we increase the size of our organization so that we change over to a HPWS?
2. How do we increase the speed with which we successfully implement HPWSs?
3. How do we maintain a HPWS so that it is sustainable through time?

A SYSTEMATIC APPROACH

The most flexible, responsive, and innovative companies will clearly dominate the next century. These qualities will not be gained through enhanced technology or massive capitalization—they will be gained only through people. HPWSs are the means to tap into this limitless asset.

As HPWSs increasingly become recognized as a distinct competitive advantage, implementation approaches that help overcome the three dilemmas will become critical. The focus of this book is to present such an approach—an approach that assures greater coverage of the organization, a faster path to positive results, and longer-term, sustainable performance.

Before we begin our journey down the implementation pathway, though, we must first understand why moving an existing organization into a HPWS is so difficult. Much of this difficulty has to do with an *enduring legacy*.

CHAPTER 2

The Enduring Legacy

Remarkable similarities exist in the way modern management is practiced in everything from the Cub Scout den meeting to the hierarchy at GM Headquarters. So pervasive is this set of common management beliefs many refer to it as the "dominant paradigm"—the set of assumptions we follow with acceptance and little question. To more fully understand how HPWSs make organizations more effective and some of the challenges associated with implementing them, we must first understand the characteristics and limitations of today's dominant management paradigm.

SEISMIC UPHEAVAL

Fueled by the aftershock of the American Revolution and the great unrest quaking across France, the 1780s marked a period of social and political upheaval that was of seismic proportions. Adding to the dynamics of this period were technical innovations, particularly in Britain, that were to become the foundation of industrialization.

The coming of industrialization gave birth to an entirely new concept of work. As factories began to emerge, the artisans and craftspersons of the period—the key producers of goods in the preindustrial era—began to be replaced by a new breed, the factory worker. The owners of these emerging organizations were suddenly faced with a host of technological and human-relations problems previously unimaginable. Since no formalized or commonly accepted set of management practices existed, the workplace was largely managed based on the whims and hunches of the owner/manager.

FROM HUNCHES TO SCIENCE

The empiricist movement which dominated British philosophy during the 1800s brought with it the first systematic examination of job design. The main implication was that work, like any other discipline from medicine to geology, could be analyzed *quantitatively* and understood from an empirical point of view. There had to be, this philosophy espoused, ways to analyze work and understand it from a rational, scientific perspective—far removed from mere guesswork. In 1832 an Englishman named Charles Babbage formally introduced a "scientific" method for performing tasks called job specialization.[1]

FRANKLIN, MARX, FREUD, AND TAYLOR

Although management through job specialization was certainly practiced throughout the 1800s, a full understanding of its potential benefits was not clear until the beginning of the twentieth century. The man responsible for heightening its popularity was an American named Frederick Winslow Taylor. In 1903 Taylor published a monumental work entitled *Shop Management*. This book, and the one that would follow eight years later entitled *Scientific Management,* had such a profound effect on the practice of management that during his own lifetime he was compared with the likes of Freud, Marx, and Franklin in terms of his impact on contemporary society.[2]

THE SCIENCE OF MANAGEMENT

Primary to Taylor's acclaimed theory, which he called "scientific management," was the notion that "every single act of every workman can be reduced to a science."[3] Taylor advocated that managers take the responsibility for gathering all the information about jobs that traditionally only the worker possessed and then classify, tabulate, and reduce this knowledge to "rules, laws, and formulae."[4] The outcome of this analysis would be the development of a standard model for performing a given job that eliminated wasted and unnecessary physical motion. The amount of time it took to perform the standardized task could then be carefully documented. In the future, any newly engineered method for accomplishing the job could be objectively compared to the former standard. If productivity was gained through the adoption of a new procedure, it would then be instituted. This suggested to Taylor and his followers that, through scientific examination, the single "best" method for performing any given job could be identified.

Taylor's works had immediate impact on American industry. "Scientific" analysis of tasks, job specialization, job simplification, and time and motion studies became dominant job design practices. It became universally accepted that such approaches were far more efficient and productive than any previous methods of management. Scientific management was particularly attractive to managers because it gave them the means to maintain direct control over the method and rate of production—control they were unable to achieve during the period when artisans and craftspersons dominated the work force. By breaking down work into simple tasks and setting performance standards for accomplishing them, management lessened the need for highly skilled employees. The complete job of the artisan, for example, could be broken down into hundreds of simple tasks. Ideally, these tasks would be so easy to learn that the training time required to become a proficient performer would be minimal. Further, if the performance of an employee fell below the acceptable standard for that job, management could simply remove him or her and bring in a replacement. Since the replacement's learning curve would be short given the simplicity of the job, the impact on production would be minimal. Overall, scientific management provided a stunning productivity advantage for employers during a period when a large percentage of the work force was immigrants with no previous experience working in factories. Additionally, the highest level of education attained for the average U.S. citizen during this period was the third grade.

By 1908, Henry Ford had translated scientific management into the context of the automobile industry. His creation of the Model T assembly line provides a vivid, early example of where American manufacturing practices were headed and how they would be carried out for the next eighty years.

Ford divided the original eighteen operations that were required to complete a unit into 7,882 operations by breaking down jobs into simple, discreet tasks. The jobs could further be characterized by the physical attributes a worker would require in order to perform them. Some jobs, for example, required "strong, able-bodied, and practically physically perfect men" while others could be filled by "women or older children."[5]

MAN AS MACHINE

Taylor associate Frank Gilberth often stated, "It is the aim of scientific management to induce men to act as nearly like machines as possible."[6] In light of the Ford example, this is strikingly clear. Ford was not concerned with the intellectual capabilities of employees—he was concerned only with their physical qualities. People became mere extensions of the machine; jobs were designed that required mechanistic, highly repetitious, machinelike behavior. If employees were unable to effectively perform their menial function, they were easily replaced. The production worker was an "expendable spare part."

The perception of "man as machine" had implications that went beyond the way the work itself was done—it also suggested where it was done. Taylor maintained that workers needed to be isolated from one another in order to eliminate any potential distractions that might be detrimental to their daily work routine. The "one man/one job principle" also applied to management interaction with the work force. According to Taylor, it was "an inflexible rule" that managers were to deal with only one employee at a time.[7]

The use of work groups and team management was not an alien idea to the business leaders of this period, though it certainly was rarely seen. Taylor himself was outspoken on the subject. He argued that when men worked in a group their individual efficiency would fall to a level below that of the worst performer. Work groups were, from Taylor's perspective, an invitation for disaster.[8]

THE FACELESS ORGANIZATION

Taylor's emphasis on employee isolation and simplifying job tasks was reinforced by Max Weber's timely introduction of the bureaucratic organization structure. Weber believed that the ideal organization would be one that was essentially faceless, where rational and impersonal decision making would be the norm. This was in vivid contrast to what he commonly observed in the various bureaus and agencies of nineteenth-century Prussia. There decision making tended to be based on such things as nepotism, friendship, and religion. Weber's answer was to create an organization that separated people into highly specialized, narrowly focused functions. Such a structure pressed against social intimacy: Individuals were focused on their specific, clearly defined, and regimented administrative duties; decisions were efficient, unbiased, and impersonal.

The marriage of scientific management and bureaucratic organization was as natural as it was seemingly inevitable. Both stressed fragmentation, narrowly defined roles and responsibilities, standardization, and central control. Both approaches had been developed as a result of observations of the failures of informal management approaches, which had been wrought with inefficiency and favoritism. Without question, the bureaucratic organization, managed by the principles of scientific management, was a stunning improvement over any previous management approach.

BACK TO THE FUTURE

In 1976 job analyst James Taylor completed a fascinating study in which he compared the current criteria used by manufacturing designers with those reported in a 1955 study. He concluded that the technological progress and innovation during the twenty-year period had little effect on the way production engineers and systems analysts designed jobs.[9] Numerous theorists have concurred that Taylor's point remains true in the 1990s. In the vast majority of companies today, jobs are designed essentially the same way they were decades ago.

Consider the following:

- A high-tech company has over five thousand job descriptions for their twenty thousand employees—on average, one out of every four workers has a completely different and unique description of specific tasks she is expected to perform.
- At United Parcel Service managers use stopwatches to time the

rate at which employees load and unload shipping trucks. Managers also "salt" the conveyer line with packages bearing incorrect addresses to check if workers are "paying attention" when loading up the trucks.

- At a major telecommunications company managers randomly listen in as operators handle customer calls. The calls are also timed to assure they are being "efficiently" handled.
- In a recent study of fifty-five U.S. plants—with an average population of 571 employees—they had an astonishing five levels of management.[10]

The list could go on and on and on. Narrowly defined jobs, standard performance rates, random performance audits, steep management hierarchy—these are but a few vestiges of Taylor's and Weber's enduring and pervasive legacy.

FIGURE 1: Control Paradigm[11]

- There is a single best way to perform any given job.

- Jobs are highly specialized and narrowly defined to ensure optimal performance of the function.

- Management sets goals, controls schedule, dictates work design, and handles administration.

- Training is focused on technical skill development.

- Rewards are based, whenever possible, on individual performance against "scientifically set" standards.

- Technological imperative: Technology and process flow are designed for optimal performance and then workers are "fit" into jobs.

- Controls are external.

- Job alienation is an accepted phenomenon of industrial life.

- Organization has a highly bureaucratic structure.

- Employees are isolated from one another to minimize distractions.

Think about your own organization for a moment.

- Are there clear status distinctions between managers and non-managers?
- Do job descriptions narrowly define the scope of work?
- Are there clearly defined standard rates at which certain tasks should be performed?
- Are offices or work stations enclosed so that interaction between employees is minimized?
- Are conference rooms relatively small so that only a handful of people can meet in them at a time?
- Are there large policy and procedure manuals?
- Is information closely guarded and handed out on a need-to-know basis?
- Are technical experts and managers the ones who typically define the way work is designed?
- Is training focused primarily on technical skills?
- Is there a steep management hierarchy?
- Are there excessive internal controls and requests for detailed information?
- Is pay based primarily on individual performance against some standard or set of measurable objectives?

If you answered yes to any of these questions, your organization has at least a few remnants of Taylor and Weber. These assumptions, practices, and structures are so pervasive I refer to them collectively as *classic management*.

THE PERVASIVE TRADITION

Why has classic management stuck with us for so long? During a period that has seen an explosion of advancements in automation, robotics, computers, and information systems—all technical innovations that are widely recognized as requiring increased work force empowerment for their potential to be realized—why has organization design changed so remarkably little? At least part of the answer is in the pervasiveness of tradition. Companies often begin relying more heavily on former experience when faced with uncertainty and change. This tendency is usually counterproductive. By reacting the same way they have in the past, companies may be addressing modern problems with obsolete solutions. This vicious cycle of addressing today's business demands by trying to do the same old things harder and faster haunts many companies.

Consider the early Eighties when predictions abounded that the personal computer (PC) would send office productivity into orbit. Today most professionals cannot imagine operating without the capabilities the PC provides. Yet during the last decade the great productivity gains that were anticipated by automating the office never appeared. In fact, the use of information technology in the service sector—where 85 percent of all information technology dollars in the U.S. are spent—has been so poor that while the dollar per employee spent on new office technology has doubled since 1982, there has been virtually no resulting productivity increase.[12] The billions of dollars in office automation have done little more than save companies from a productivity decline! In fact, because of the extraordinary capital expenditure required to buy the latest hardware, software, peripherals, and networking capabilities, a case can be made that many firms would have been financially stronger and just as productive if they had simply ignored the computer revolution altogether and kept their electric typewriters and Roladexs!

DISASTER SPIRAL

While companies were spending billions on the latest technology, they largely ignored the people side of the equation, assuming that minor adjustments to past management practices would be enough to ensure success. As failures were experienced, the

FIGURE 2: Disaster Spiral

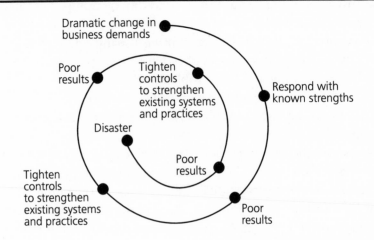

reaction was to further enforce and strengthen existing management systems and controls. As more failures were experienced, the general reaction was still the same—strengthen existing controls and systems. A spiral of disaster had formed, resulting in a productivity failure of staggering proportions.

This cycle is a difficult one to break since it is undeniable that classic management has served many companies quite well for decades. After all, if you're a baseball player and having trouble hitting, isn't the answer to go back to the fundamentals? Why wouldn't the same be true of a company? If market share is slipping or productivity is down or you're having difficulty implementing a new technology, isn't it a good time to get back to basics? The flaw in this perspective is that the nature of the game for many companies has completely changed. Improving your hitting does little good if the sport you are now playing is basketball. For many organizations the nature of the game and the specific skills needed to excel in the marketplace are changing almost daily.

While it remains true that the bureaucratic organization, managed by the principles of scientific management, is the unshakable cornerstone of organizational design in the Western world, it has also become clear to many businesses and institutions that their problems cannot be answered by working harder and faster using the same old management assumptions and practices. Unquestionably, classic management has served us well. Consider the dramatic productivity improvements experienced throughout this century as clear evidence of the profound power of the Taylor/Weber philosophy. But in the context of the 1990s this same philosophy has become a great inhibitor to progress.

THE GREAT INHIBITORS

Many of the strengths of classic management in the bygone eras of the Forties, Fifties, Sixties, and even Seventies now serve as the greatest weaknesses in the turbulence of the Nineties. Nowhere is this more evident than in the emphasis on inflexible systems that slow responsiveness (the adaptation crisis), narrowly defined jobs that treat employees like machines (the expendable spare human), and extensive departments and rigid hierarchical structures filled with red tape and politics (the iron bureaucracy). These characteristics, inherent in classic management, inhibit organization effectiveness in two profound ways:

1. They limit how quickly the organization can adapt to change.
2. They serve to create enormous pockets of resistance that stunt the efforts of would-be reformers.

THE ADAPTATION CRISIS

In 1980 when GM owned 46 percent of the U.S. car market, few would have predicted that its share would plummet to barely 35 percent by the decade's end.[13] Most analysts attribute this market-share free-fall to a public that, unable to forget the poor quality of the late Seventies and early Eighties, had simply changed their buying habits.

Over the last several years the emphasis on getting quality programs in place among corporations has been extraordinary—and how could it be otherwise? Who is going to argue with the desire to create a product or provide a service that is of *total quality*? And yet many companies have abandoned their quality efforts after watching them miserably fail. Abandon quality—preposterous! Yet the conclusions of a recent study demonstrate just how widespread *quality abandonment* has become. Thirty-eight percent of senior managers at ninety-five corporations said their quality efforts had failed in one recent study. In a separate study, conducted by Arthur D. Little, only 36 percent of the five hundred executives surveyed believed their company's quality efforts had helped improve their competitiveness.[14] The failure of many of these efforts has brought with it predictable cynicism. At the McDonnell Douglas commercial airplane division, many refer to the acronym TQMS (intended to stand for Total Quality Management Systems) as meaning Time to Quit and Move to Seattle (Seattle is the location of Boeing Corporation, McDonnell Douglas's highly successful competitor).

What GM and McDonnell Douglas and a host of other corporations are facing is the *adaptation crisis*. The playing field for their respective businesses has profoundly changed while the inner workings of their organizations have changed little. They are structured for control, not nimbleness and flexibility. Implementing a new quality approach becomes a painful ordeal because it invariably runs counter to a host of existing systems and processes—many of which current managers have a strong vested interest in maintaining as they are.

The central issue for most organizations today is adaptation—not control. Rather than developing systems and methods to permanently control and stabilize processes and procedures, the emphasis shifts toward being responsive and proactive. Today

FIGURE 3: Control vs. Adaptation

Traditional Perspective	Emerging Perspective
Control is central to effective management.	*Adaptation* to change is central to effective management.
Assumption:	**Assumption:**
The business environment is relatively placid and changes in a slow, predictable manner.	The business environment is changing at a phenomenal rate and in ways that are often difficult to predict.

competitive advantage is often gained by being able to respond to changes in technology, markets, or regulations faster than the competition. As a result, modern managers have the difficult task of focusing much of their time and attention on understanding and preparing their organizations for change rather than overseeing and enforcing existing rules and procedures.

Classic management puts such an emphasis on control that it often trivializes the importance of adaptation and responsiveness. Key aspects of increasing organization responsiveness, such as decentralization and increasing the autonomy of work groups, are often seen as running counter to maintaining strong management control. In this way classic management limits the organization's ability to adapt to changing conditions.

THE EXPENDABLE SPARE HUMAN

Look at the mission statement of nearly any corporation and you will find some variation of the theme "Our employees are our most valuable asset." While everyone says these words, few companies actually put them to practice. Since it was the intent of scientific management to entice workers to act as much like machines as possible, it is not surprising that most policies and practices are designed to do exactly that. Being treated like a machine does little for a person's self-esteem, participation, or personal development.

In corporations today people are treated as machines in two significant ways. First, the design of work has typically been narrowly defined, specialized, and highly repetitious. A factory worker's job might be to tighten a particular screw as it passes on the assembly line; for a secretary it might be spending each day typing documents into a word processor. Second, people tend to be viewed as inanimate and even expendable parts. They become "head count" and "overhead costs."

This perception often leads to decisions that, in retrospect, seem utter nonsense. In the 1970s and early 1980s Sears, in a move to lower aggregate wage and substantially cut benefit costs, shifted the composition of its sales force from 70 percent full-time to 70 percent part-timers. While the move did initially serve to cut costs, it led to increased turnover and a dramatic drop in customer satisfaction.[15] While it is difficult to put an exact figure on the cost to Sears resulting from the loss of so many customers, it is safe to bet that it far exceeded the initial savings gained from restructuring the sales force. In fact, the cost of turnover alone may have exceeded the initial savings. Merck & Company has found that turnover costs them one and a half times an employee's annual salary because of disruptions to working relationships and the transactional costs of getting employees on and off the payroll (not to mention training costs and productivity losses as the new employee "comes up to speed").[16]

As employees come to recognize that they are little more than cogs in a great corporate wheel, their degree of frustration and detachment increases. In the extreme, the results can be tragic and include problems like high absenteeism, product sabotage, alcoholism, drug abuse, and poor health.

Most corporations, despite the flowery words in their mission statements, treat employees consistent with the biases of classic management—as if they were machines. People are viewed as a way to support technology and not as a significant competitive asset in their own right. Today competitive advantage is rarely—if ever—gained by improving technology alone. Eventually everyone has access to the same pool of technological know-how. Competitive advantage can be gained only through employees—employees who are more responsive, flexible, creative, informed, committed, and customer-oriented than those of their competitors. Here the prevailing wisdom of classic management fails miserably—it runs completely counter to gaining competitive advantage through the development of people.

THE IRON BUREAUCRACY

The expression "The right hand doesn't know what the left hand is doing" is all too common in organizations today. Often this is the result of extensive, narrowly defined departments that, through their very structure, press against coordination and interdependency.

To dramatically illustrate the point, consider the story of former Oregon Governor Tom McCall. When he took office he had been directly involved with state government for over two decades as a journalist covering the inner workings of the legislature, and later as an assistant to two governors. He was, upon the day he took office, one of the best-prepared individuals ever to ascend to the governorship of the state.

McCall writes in his autobiography that there were 175 agencies, boards, and commissions he knew of when he became governor. Through careful analysis, about a hundred more were soon discovered. He goes on to write:

> I appointed a special study group . . . to investigate the ways and means of reorganization. . . . Their analysis uncovered agencies,

boards and commissions that previous governors had never heard of. They revealed that the governor was chairman of the State Power Agency. I had been intimately involved with Oregon's government for 20 years and never even knew it existed.[17]

What McCall had discovered was a mature bureaucracy. Responsibility, accountability, and mission for many of the organizations within Oregon's government had dissipated through the years. Departments created to address urgent problems continued to live long after the intent of their original charter. Meanwhile, new departments were created to address new problems. The structure grew and grew until it literally was out of control.

While it is often acknowledged that governments, whether they are at the federal, state, county, or city level, are overly bureaucratic, slow to respond, and inefficient, there is an underlying feeling that the private sector is exempt from these same problems. The unsaid assumption is that the free-market system, with its emphasis on competitiveness, assures that only effective, progressive organizations survive. Many managers in the private sector are openly critical of their governmental counterparts, playing off the stereotype that the bastion of ineffective organization design and management practice is isolated in governmental institutions. This belief, what might be called "organizational Darwinism," is simply not substantiated by the facts. Inefficient bureaucracy (or what some are referring to as "corpocracy"), misguided management, political combat—it is all as rampant in the private sector as it is in the public. Both, after all, are manifestations of the same underlying philosophy of classic management.

Richard Palermo, vice president for Quality and Transition at Xerox, notes, "If a problem has been bothering your company and your customers for years and won't yield, that problem is the result of a cross-functional dispute, where nobody has total control of the whole process."[18] Such disputes are common and often perpetuated by managers who have little understanding or familiarity with neighboring departments. Most senior executives, for example, stay within the same function their entire career. Those who started their careers in the finance department, for instance, will probably never move outside of that sphere. This creates a kind of *functional myopia* where the world is viewed through the eyes of unique specialties. As one engineering manager noted, "My people are concerned and focused on their profession far more than they are on the company or our customers—those are strictly secondary concerns."

The requirements placed on organizations to effectively coordinate interdependent yet unique areas of specialization have become extraordinary. Sun Microsystems, Inc., a leader in computer work stations, has already introduced eight generations of products in its nine and a half years of existence and recognizes that it must increase the pace in the future. Fisher Controls, a leader in computerized control systems, is attempting to streamline its development process so that it has a major system release every single year. The only way such dramatic time-to-market figures can be achieved is by dissolving the artificial barriers that exist between departments and groups.

Whether one is attempting to increase productivity, quality, service responsiveness, or time-to-market, the need for the effective integration of various specialized skills increases. Classic management's emphasis on isolation of specialists acts against this need for integration and serves to perpetuate increased bureaucracy and political infighting.

A FIRESTORM OF DIFFICULTY

These are the key limitations of classic management: the failure to adapt and respond to change; the failure to utilize the full potential of human assets; and the failure to integrate knowledge and expertise. In sharp contrast, HPWSs stress teamwork and flexible organization structures, broad work roles and responsibilities, shared authority and responsibility, and the open sharing of information. The friction between these two extremes can ignite a firestorm of difficulty when attempting to implement a team-based approach into an existing organization. In Chapter 3 we will begin our exploration of how to overcome these predictable sources of resistance to change.

CHAPTER **3**

The Transformation
Pathway

■ *While working in Kodak's International Operations, Ralph Olney[1] had the opportunity to broaden his perspectives of not only the film business, but of U.S. industry in general. He had witnessed dramatic competitive changes in a variety of markets and could see the traumatic impact they were having on many corporations. The experience left him a changed person. Upon returning to Kodak's main headquarters in Rochester, New York, to become manager of 13 Room—the manufacturing area that produces professional and commercial color film—Olney wanted to use his new perspective and create an organization that was second to none. He recognized that this would require a management team that was selflessly committed to transferring their knowledge and expertise to those who worked with them. During one of his early meetings with the managers, he matter-of-factly stated, "Let's figure out a way to work ourselves out of our jobs."*

■ *When Don Bell asked the plant managers of Monsanto's Fiber Operations for a 50 percent increase in productivity, nervous silence filled the room. Had Bell gone completely crackers? Nothing remotely close to that kind of improvement had ever been achieved in Fibers. Bell himself had only a vague idea of how it could be accomplished. He recognized that the change would require a new and fundamentally different management approach—one that engendered an extraordinary level of involvement and commitment among all employees. As the transition began to unfold, Bell was encouraged by the receptiveness of managers and employees to the changes he was advocating. There was far less resistance than he had anticipated. It was as if he had discovered a pathway that, when followed, seemed to increase the speed and level acceptance for the change effort. And, as he reviewed the initial results, it became obvious that it was a pathway that led to vastly superior performance.*

■ *Fred Hanson, vice president and general manager of Tektronix's Portable Oscilloscope Division, sat looking over the most recent month's results. A smile broke across his face as he reviewed the profit and loss statement—the numbers were astonishing. He leaned back in his chair reflecting on what had happened over the last two years, a period that had seen his division go from being the company's number-one financial loser to being its greatest profit contributor. It was a transition that had seen fundamental changes in the way the organization operated, including the implementation of high performance work teams. In hindsight there were many things Hanson would have done differently, but overall it was remarkable how smooth the transition had gone. "What can be taken from our success," he wondered, "and applied to other organizations?"*

THE TRANSFORMATION PATHWAY

Implementing a HPWS requires a complete transformation of the workplace—virtually all systems, processes, structures, and roles are re-created. Without strong management support and a systematic implementation approach, the effort is virtually guaranteed failure.

While there is no step-by-step recipe for implementing HPWSs, there is a pathway that, when followed, greatly increases

FIGURE 4: The Transformation Pathway

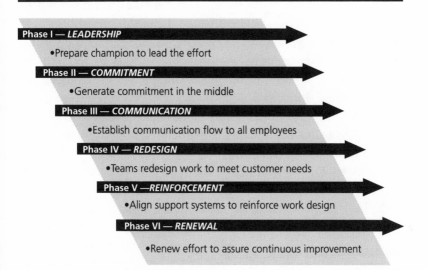

Phase I — *LEADERSHIP*
•Prepare champion to lead the effort

Phase II — *COMMITMENT*
•Generate commitment in the middle

Phase III — *COMMUNICATION*
•Establish communication flow to all employees

Phase IV — *REDESIGN*
•Teams redesign work to meet customer needs

Phase V —*REINFORCEMENT*
•Align support systems to reinforce work design

Phase VI — *RENEWAL*
•Renew effort to assure continuous improvement

the likelihood of success. It is called the Transformation Pathway and to follow it—as Olney, Bell, and Hanson did—requires progression through six critical phases.

1. *Leadership.* The first phase of the transition focuses on getting a sponsor or champion in place who will support the change. There must be someone who can articulate why the change is important to the organization and who can provide a vision of where the organization needs to go. The individual needs a working knowledge of HPWSs; clout to make change happen through his ability to influence; and a clear sense of the concerns and aspirations of the people within the organization he is attempting to transform.

2. *Commitment.* In this phase, the effort is expanded to include key opinion leaders within the organization. Initially their efforts focus on clarifying the connection between HPWSs and overall business strategy. The opinion leaders then become

actively involved in planning out the change process and begin recognizing how their roles—and the roles of others within the organization—will be affected during the transition.

3. *Communication.* The third phase stresses altering the flow of information in order to expand its accessibility to nearly everyone in the organization. Often this means dismantling the hierarchical information pathway, restructuring reports, and reassessing what information should be considered "confidential." As teams begin using the expanded flow of information, problem solving expands.

4. *Redesign.* During this phase, focus is on improving the design of the entire organization. Teams take an active role in the redesign process, focusing on such things as how to streamline processes, improve quality, lessen functional barriers, and expand roles. At this point in the transition the organization has begun to alter the way it operates—many procedures, workflow processes, and roles have dramatically changed.

5. *Reinforcement.* Next, support systems (such as the compensation system and other internal, corporate systems) are the focus of reform. The intent is to make changes to the support systems so that they reinforce and strengthen the emerging HPWS design.

6. *Renewal.* In the final phase, the emphasis is on sustaining energy and enthusiasm at a level that assures continuous performance improvement.

MAKING THE TRANSITION

Monsanto's Fiber Operations, an organization encompassing four different manufacturing plants, used employee involvement as the foundation for dramatically improving operational performance. Spurred on by a vision of the "Plant of the Nineties," Monsanto introduced a series of changes that have left the fiber operations business significantly altered, in effect *transformed.*

Tektronix, seeing a marked decline in their portable oscilloscope business, introduced HPWSs as a way to turn around performance. Kodak's 13 Room, feeling the bombardment of Fuji film in its marketplace, used HPWTs as part of its strategy to improve quality and lower costs. Each of these cases provides insight into how an organization can effectively utilize the Transformation Pathway in making the transition from classic management to a high performance work system.

THE LEADERSHIP PHASE

Where does organization change begin? At its genesis, there is a single individual, or a small group of individuals, who are the champions for change. Through their leadership, awareness within the organization builds—people begin to recognize why the change is necessary and the potential benefits that could be gained from it.

There are two primary outcomes of this phase: First, a champion or group of champions who are advocating the transition to HPWSs is identified. Often they self-select; this was clearly the case with Monsanto's Don Bell and Kodak's Ralph Olney. In other instances the champion is developed through the efforts of other members in the organization who lack the legitimate authority to effectively lead the change, but whose advice is readily listened to by those who can.

Second, the champion(s) clearly communicates why it is important for the organization to make the transition to HPWSs. Typically this includes a *case for change* and a *vision of new possibilities* for the organization.

Case for Change

It has been long recognized that the status quo or routine pattern of an organization must be disrupted or "unfrozen" before it can undergo substantive change. This unfreezing event, or series of events, can take on many forms—it can be the result of disastrous business performance, a major restructuring, dramatic growth, or the implementation of a new technology. For the champion, the case for change is a tool to help the unfreezing begin.

Often the case for change is no more than a five-minute description that clearly depicts:

1. Why the change is important
2. What is likely to happen if the change does not occur
3. In what ways people involved in the change, as well as the organization as a whole, are likely to benefit from it

The sophistication of the case for change is far less important than how widely understood it becomes within the organization. A lengthy, analytical treatise will have far less impact than a series of informal presentations and regular discussions. One of the remarkable features at Tektronix was how employees, irrespective of their level in the management hierarchy, would describe the case for change using nearly identical words. It was a universal, commonly accepted expression of the challenges the division faced.

In 1983, Hanson began describing the case for change to his staff with a Gary Larson cartoon. The cartoon depicted a stegosaurus at a podium talking to an audience of fellow dinosaurs. The caption read, "The picture is pretty bleak, gentlemen. The world's climates are changing, the mammals are taking over and we all have a brain about the size of a walnut."[2] After the laughing had subsided, Hanson explained that the division had become much like a dinosaur. It had great size and strength, but this was quickly becoming its nemesis rather than its advantage. What had worked in the past—and worked very well—was far different than what would be required for survival in the future.

This case for change was further accentuated by some startling statistics showing that Japanese oscilloscope exports worldwide had nearly doubled from 1978 to 1983 while Tektronix's oscilloscope sales had remained essentially flat. The financial performance of the division was no less startling in 1983, showing a loss of $23 million in that year. Hanson explained that without a dramatic turnaround Tektronix would be out of the portable-oscilloscope business and a thousand people would be out of work. He went on to describe how he believed the turnaround could be achieved, focusing first on major initiatives in manufacturing (Just-in-Time and Material Requirements Planning) and engineering (reduced product development times and Design for Manufacturability). These initiatives, he recognized, could only be achieved by dramatic changes in the very practice of management. The creation of a HPWS would be the foundation on which all the other changes would stand.

It was becoming clear in the mid-1980s within Monsanto's Fiber Operations that performance was slipping relative to the competition. Bell became outspoken about the issue, noting that without some significant change, lost market share and plant closures looked inevitable. At Kodak, Olney was very clear about the threat other film companies—particularly Fuji—posed for Kodak. In both instances, as the case for change became more widely recognized, it helped strengthen the convictions of management that it needed to make manufacturing performance a strategic weapon.

Developing a Vision and Creating New Possibilities

Few deny that having a clear vision of their organization's direction is important, yet few organizations are truly guided by a vision of the future. Daily, operational needs typically take precedence over more strategic, long-term, and "visionary" activities, leaving most managers on a treadmill of slow, incremental improvement. Implementing HPWSs requires a leader who is capable of describing what the organization could become with enough clarity and direction that people find it something they can truly aspire to.

Don Bell introduced two simple goals shortly after he became General Manager of Fiber Operations for Monsanto. They were:

1. A 50 percent productivity increase over the course of the next three years
2. The full integration of Total Quality Management on the shop floor

The goals had profound implications and were initially dismissed by some as "unachievable." One manager even confessed that he thought Bell was "out of touch with reality" by even suggesting such stunning levels of improvement.

By stating these goals and demonstrating his commitment to seeing them achieved, Bell had disrupted the mental groove of the managers in his organization. The changes needed to achieve such a significant productivity improvement could not be incremental as they had been in the past. The 3 to 5 percent improvement per year was a mere fraction of the goal he wanted to achieve. There had to be a step function improvement, a breakthrough, a totally different orientation than the organization's current direction. It required throwing out old solutions. The very thinking about the way the organization operated and what was possible had to be altered.

Over the course of the next nine months, a team was formed of key contributors from each of the four plants that made up Fiber Operations. The team's mission was to explore new concepts for improving business performance. From their work emerged a new vision of the workplace: a workplace that had a completely integrated manufacturing strategy consisting of total quality, computer-integrated manufacturing (CIM), and employee involvement. In such an organization productivity would be tripled, quality near perfect, the latest technologies effectively utilized, profits very strong, and employee satisfaction high. This vision became known as the "Plant of the Nineties."

THE COMMITMENT PHASE

The Commitment Phase is characterized by its emphasis on getting key opinion leaders within the organization "on board" with the change—an often daunting task. Managers, largely trained on the assumptions, models, and systems of classic management, often find the concepts associated with HPWSs difficult to understand and even more difficult to put into operation. Experience suggests that some, even the best intended, never fully recognize how to implement and perpetuate high-involvement practices. These managers simply cannot make the "mental leap." Their thinking about the practice of management is so deeply ingrained, their assumptions and practices so habitual, that to change, regardless of how logical or rational the argument to do so, is very difficult.

The strategy for gaining the support of these key opinion leaders—defined as the people without whose support the transition to HPWSs will likely fail—is simple: Get them involved. Use their active participation in developing the implementation blueprint as the vehicle to gain their commitment.

Olney's strategy for getting the 13 Room supervisors directly involved in the transition was making his staff into a study group. Starting in June, they met one or two days every month to discuss one of the twelve books that they had jointly decided were the "essentials" in understanding HPWSs. During their discussions they would note specific concepts, ideas, or models that were directly applicable to their operation. (Their observations from the readings later became the foundation for the vision, operating principles, and many of the strategies that were specified in the 13 Room business plan.) The study group continued until all the books had been analyzed (a period lasting five months).

Upon completion of the study sessions, the staff developed a vision and the operating principles for 13 Room. The vision they developed looked three to five years into the future and was focused on five areas of responsibility: site, management systems, operations, personnel, and planning. To further the role expansion of the first-level supervisors, each of Olney's five supervisors became responsible for managing one of these areas in addition to maintaining their regular manufacturing responsibilities. The supervisor responsible for personnel, for example, developed the group's affirmative-action goals, determined training needs, assured conformance to state and federal laws with regard to labor practices, and oversaw the compensation program. The supervisors regarded the chance to absorb these responsibilities as being "exciting opportunities" rather than "just more work." As one supervisor succinctly put it, "I was having fun for the first time in years."

In assessing current organization structure, the management team determined that it was a hindrance to information sharing and problem solving. Under the proposed reorganization, teams would be formed based on the flow of the product. (Formerly teams had been formed and managed based on their shift.) When later implemented, the new structure created some immediate advantages, including far greater visibility of bottlenecks and problem areas. It also had the advantage of creating a stronger sense of team identity among the operators.

THE COMMUNICATION PHASE

To a large extent the Leadership and Commitment phases are preparatory in nature—they establish a strong foundation for the transition but do little to actually change any of the systems, structures, processes, or roles within the organization. By contrast, the Communication Phase begins focusing on altering these core elements. The outcomes of this phase reflect this emphasis:

- Establish methods for sharing regular business information (including general information as well as specific, operational information) and for obtaining continuous feedback.

- Provide clarity of how roles will expand (this includes management, specialists, supervisors, and work team members).
- Provide necessary training and education opportunities to assure that needed skill sets and abilities are developing.

Up the Information Elevator

Traditionally, information has gone up the management hierarchy to where decisions were made and then back down to where they were implemented. The assumption was that decision making was the responsibility of management and the execution of decisions was the responsibility of those lower in the organization.

HPWSs represent a dramatic departure from this "elevator approach." In a HPWS information should go to the point where direct action can be taken. Information, decision making, and the implementation of the decision should reside at the point closest to where the work is actually being performed. It should not be separated by hierarchy, status, or other artificial barriers. Naturally, for such a decentralized method of decision making to work, there must be adequate, easily accessible information provided to employees at all levels. In addition, employees must have a broad understanding of the business to assure that their team's decisions will not have a negative impact on the overall operation.

The Awareness Transfer

Fred Hanson found himself with a significant dilemma when he joined Tektronix in 1983. Before him was an organization with tremendous potential, yet in the last fiscal year it had been operating well into the red. To make matters worse, there was no sense of urgency—the organization seemed to plod along to the tune "Don't Worry, Be Happy."

The problem, he soon realized, was that virtually no one in the organization below his staff had any idea that the organization was in dire straits. People naturally assumed that everything was fine, just as it always had been. At this point Hanson made the decision to begin monthly assemblies where he would review the division's income statement and the highlights of the discussions among his staff with everyone in the organization. It would be his attempt at an "awareness transfer."

When his peers in other divisions of the company first heard about his idea, many were skeptical, while others thought it was just plain dangerous. By giving everyone in the organization access to the income statement, they warned, the sales and profit information would certainly make it into the hands of competitors. Others suggested that by "telling all," employees would be unmotivated, thinking more about the possibility of layoffs than about performing their jobs. "You must protect them [the work force] from this kind of thing," recommended one senior manager.

Undaunted, Hanson played out his convictions, believing that "telling all" was the best strategy for coalescing commitment and support. Due to the size of the division—about four hundred employees—he held several sessions so he could keep the group size to between thirty and forty employees. The small groups assured lively discussions. For many employees it was their first sense of the total business, from customer needs to engineering design to manufacturing to marketing and sales.

Complete Visibility

Having some sense of the context of the business is important for employees if they are to broaden their perspective of the organization and its direction. This awareness needs to be further complemented by operational information that gives service providers, operators, and technicians greater knowledge of the performance of their work unit. A lack of information stunts any meaningful development of problem-solving groups. Without adequate information, problem solving is unfocused and typically not tied to the relevant business problems.

Introducing operational information into the workplace can be done as simply as sharing graphs that chart the quality and productivity performance of the group or with as much complexity as introducing a computer-integrated manufacturing (CIM) strategy. Regardless of the complexity of the system used to convey it, relevant operational information must be readily accessible.

The implementation of CIM by Monsanto's Fiber Operations provided a tremendous amount of previously unavailable information to those working on the shop floor. Since the implementation of CIM had been tied with HPWS concepts, it naturally followed that the system would allow operators and technicians to instantly access information relating to the performance of current processes and use this information to make the necessary adjustments to improve output and quality.

The potential of CIM—and other computer-integrated information systems—is often not realized because many managers fail to see the relationship between the accessibility of information and the potential of high performance management practices. Introducing CIM, and then maintaining a rigid management structure that denies operators the ability to utilize the information in a meaningful way, is a terrible waste of the system's potential and the people using it. Monsanto's enlightened view has created a system where operators are empowered to take direct action based on the information they receive.

The Information Sunrise

In HPWSs, information is a tool and not a privilege. Everyone in the organization must have access to the maximum amount of information that is reasonable to be able to assimilate, understand, and utilize. The information elevator must be replaced by a kind of "information sunrise" where, like rays of sun spreading across the horizon, everyone in the organization—not just a few high-ranking managers—is privy to key information and is able to manipulate it for decision making.

New Roles for a New Workplace

Increasing the accessibility of information has obvious implications on work roles and the skill sets employees need to develop. During the Communication Phase, managers and team members are introduced to a new set of competencies they will need to develop as members of a HPWS.

The question arises in virtually all efforts to introduce HPWSs: "What happens to managers and supervisors? How does their role change?" Often the role of supervisors in high performance organizations is described in terms of the specific responsibilities they should be turning over to the team. The list of responsibilities the manager will acquire is typically filled with ambiguous clichés like "coach," "leader," and "facilitator." Often these terms are not helpful to managers who find themselves struggling with how they should be spending their time and where they should be focusing their energies. As a result, many supervisors faced with the transition to high performance practices have a fairly concrete notion of what they should be giving up, but only an abstract idea of their new role. The supervisory role appears to be constricting, getting smaller and smaller until the work team is doing everything that was formerly the manager's responsibility.

Certainly as the work group matures it can (and should) continually absorb responsibilities that were formerly the sole bastion of management. However, in well-constructed implementation efforts the expansion of the group's role should not mean a contraction of the management role. As teams are able to take on more of the traditional management duties (e.g., hiring new employees, monitoring attendance, filling out quality and output reports, determining the most effective work flow, directly addressing customer concerns), managers are in a position to begin expanding the realm of their own roles. Managers are able to increase their interaction with customers and vendors, take a more active role in exploring new technologies that are likely to impact their team, and spend more time working on strategic issues and long-term planning. In effect, a lot of the day-to-day "fire fighting" that often consumes the majority of supervisory time becomes lessened as the work team matures. This, in turn, frees up supervisors and managers to expand their role into areas that are essential for gaining and maintaining a competitive advantage in the marketplace. Simply, the transition to HPWSs represents an opportunity for role expansion among team members, supervisors, and managers. As a manufacturing manager at Tektronix noted, "Finally I'm contributing the way I should be—I'm adding value and not baby-sitting."

THE REDESIGN PHASE

The momentum created by expanding the flow of information and establishing new role expectations propels the organization into the Redesign Phase of the effort. Armed with their broadened awareness of the business and their work area, employees begin to recognize that many of the problems they face daily—whether related to productivity, cost, service, quality, safety, or job satisfaction—are a direct result of the way the work and work roles were designed. Some of these work design problems force employees into jobs that are difficult to perform. Others were created by ineffective or out-of-date equipment or a work flow that requires excessive material handling and time-consuming documentation that adds significant cost but no value. As these problems emerge, it is critical that the work team becomes directly involved in redesigning the way work is performed.

Groups tend to design their work in a way that best optimizes the needs of the individual with the technology necessary to perform the job. This suggests that healthy and productive work environments can be created by assuring that those actually performing the work are directly involved in its design and continuous redesign.

In conducting a work redesign, teams must examine three critical elements:

1. The current environment facing the organization
2. The technical system (e.g., equipment, process flow, furniture, physical setting)
3. The social system (e.g., management practices, work roles, relationships, rewards)

The demands of the external environment can take many forms, including changes in customer expectations, new government regulations, a shortage of qualified job applicants, or increased competitive pressures. Once these challenges are clearly understood, the internal workings of the organization are analyzed to see how they are helping or hindering to meet them. Based on this analysis, a redesign is developed that, ideally, puts the organization in a superior position to respond to the challenges and opportunities it faces.

FIGURE 5: The Redesign Process

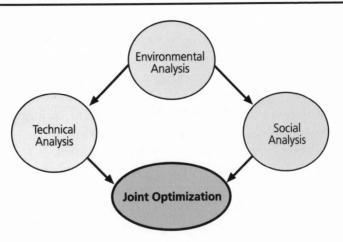

THE REINFORCEMENT PHASE

The objective of the Reinforcement Phase is to strengthen the emerging HPWS design. This is accomplished by aligning the various support systems with the new design. Among the first priorities is to establish an effective ongoing training and development program.

Fiber Operations employees at Monsanto were spending from 10 to 20 percent of their work time in training where they developed new job skills and acquired knowledge relevant to operating in a team environment. The figures within the Portable Oscilloscope Division and 13 Room were similar (10 to 15 percent). In all three cases the amount of training hours more than doubled following the introduction of HPWSs. Less obvious, but equally important, were the changes required to such things as the accounting system, the maintenance function, and the role of the corporate staff. Failure of these and other key support groups to change their operation in a way that is complementary to the requirements of HPWSs will stunt the organization's overall development.

Rewards—particularly the compensation system—must also change in order to effectively sustain the HPWS design. At Tektronix representatives from the shop floor along with representatives from management and Human Resources designed an entirely new compensation system for the portable oscilloscope business. Monsanto's Chocolate Bayou and Greenwood plants recognized that their two-tier compensation and benefits packages were inconsistent with their new HPWS environment. Both plants aggressively pursued creating an all-salaried work force in order to eliminate these artificial barriers. In addition, Monsanto has given its business unit managers a tremendous amount of flexibility in determining the appropriate pay system for their individual organization. This has created a fertile environment for experimentation in alternative reward structures, including pay for knowledge, lump-sum bonuses, profit sharing, gain sharing, and "cafeteria style" benefit packages.

While there is agreement that informal rewards (such as verbal reinforcement to the work teams from top management, coverage in the company newsletter, etc.) must begin during the earliest stages of the transition, there is considerable debate about the best time to make fundamental changes to the pay system or other formal reward systems (such as the benefits package). Some argue that these changes should occur early—that a new pay system should, in effect, lead the change effort. The rationale is simple: People will ultimately do what they are paid to do. If the compensation system rewards people for acting like team members, then people will begin acting like team members.

If this viewpoint seems overly simplistic, well, it is. There are numerous factors that affect behavior in the workplace, many of which affect it far more profoundly than pay. The perspective that employees do only what they are paid to do is a vestige of classic management that has simply failed to die even as our understanding of organizations has increased. Experience shows that compensation should be among the last systems to undergo change.[3]

THE RENEWAL PHASE

In effective transitions to HPWSs, there is sustained performance improvement. In the case of the Portable Oscilloscope Division, the sustained performance lasted over four years. Then things begin to change. "I just don't understand it," reported an operator. "After years of improvements, everything just seems to be slowing down. It is as if we're in slow motion." Indeed, the improvement trends in output, quality, lead time, and on-time delivery had all flattened. The manufacturing manager of the division referred to the slowdown as "organization morass"—it was as if there was some mysterious barrier the organization had suddenly hit.

Hyper-Criticality and the Invincibility Complex

After expending tremendous energy to progress through the first five phases of the effort, it may seem unfair that in the final phase of the transition improvement trends often begin to flatten. After years of dramatic improvement a team may suddenly find itself plateauing—the rate of improvement remaining essentially flat. The origin of the "plateau phenomenon" exists within the collective psychology of the team itself. In some cases it is the result of frustrations that the team is not living up to its potential. Members of effective high performing teams will often develop enormous expectations of what the team can achieve and may become highly critical of the team's performance when certain goals are not met. Nothing the team does is "quite good enough" or "near what we're capable of." In the extreme, an atmosphere of *hyper-criticality* is created to the point where it can actually become crippling to sustained team performance.

Another source of team plateauing can come from excessive glorification of past accomplishments. Teams can become overconfident in their own abilities and put such a value on past accomplishments that they begin to lose perspective on the importance of continuous improvement. They develop an "invincibility mentality": "No one can touch us." While confidence and recognition of past accomplishments are important (a member of one manufacturing team told me, "We are the elite, the best, the Marine Corps of teams"), obsession with them can lead to a lack of focus on the requirements for success in the future.

The objective of the Renewal Phase is to help the team sustain its energy and cohesion so that continuous improvement remains unending. For teams suffering from hyper-criticality, some of the specific techniques used to help re-focus them include celebrating their past accomplishments and helping them recognize their level of improvement relative to comparable teams in other companies. For teams who see themselves as "invincible" when the facts seem to clearly show otherwise, the emphasis is on establishing benchmarks from the best comparable organizations they can use in assessing their current performance; reassessment of the current competitive pressures facing the organization; and establishing a team vision of greatness that looks out three to five years into the future.

A "PULL" FOR CHANGE

The potential competitive advantage gained through HPWSs is great. Consider the fiber operations plants where productivity soared to the 40 to 50 percent range in just three years. In addition, costs were substantially down, quality up, and job satisfaction high. In the Portable Oscilloscope Division the figures were no less impressive: a 20 percent improvement in quality (based on their internal corporate audit), a 75 percent decrease in inventory, and a 50 percent improvement in productivity over a five-year period. In two years 13 Room scored a 27 percent quality improvement, a 67 percent increase in safety, an 11 percent decrease in cost, and the highest rating of any production unit in the Film Sensitizing Division's annual quality of work life survey.

The power of the sequence is in how it creates a natural "pull" for change. Each phase helps build momentum and strength for the phase that immediately follows. Contrasted with a "push" approach, where people are directed when and how to change, a "pull" is characterized by creating opportunities for people to participate in the effort. People choose to experiment with new systems, processes, and roles as a way to help improve the organization's performance—they don't feel tricked or coerced into supporting the effort.

The Transformation Pathway serves as a vital framework for those interested in improving their organization's level of empowerment and overall performance. To successfully progress through each phase requires a combination of vision, skill, perseverance, and patience. The potential benefits to the organization are great, as are the potential risks.

PART TWO

Recreating the Workplace

*I*t must be remembered there is nothing more difficult to plan, more doubtful of success, nor dangerous to manage than the creation of a new system. For the initiator has the enmity of all who would profit by the preservation of the old institution and merely lukewarm defenders in those who would gain by the new one. . . . Thus it arises that on every opportunity to attack reformers, opponents do so with the zeal of partisans, the others only defend them halfheartedly.

From *The Prince*
by Machiavelli, 1513

CHAPTER 4

The Making of a Champion

In 1991 IBM recorded the first loss in its long and illustrious history. The dismal performance sent shock waves throughout the business community. The infallible giant was suddenly losing its market dominance. Drowning in overpriced products, excessive overhead costs, a relative lack of new offerings, and a dwindling service reputation, the company was in a sea of tumultuous turmoil.

A NEW IBM

The remedy? A new IBM. An IBM that will be flexible and highly responsive to the market. An IBM with less hierarchy and more autonomy granted to local units. An IBM dominated by teams and teamwork. The call for change was clear, and nowhere in the corporation was the response more immediate and dramatic than in Canada. In March 1992, IBM Canada president and CEO Bill Etherington accurately observed, "It is reasonable to state that IBM Canada has experienced more change over the past one hundred days or so than at any time in the company's seventy-five-year history."[1]

The one hundred days had seen a major restructuring and a corresponding flattening of the hierarchy, the introduction of a team achievement plan, an increase in the level of autonomy of the sales and service branches, a heavy emphasis on high performance teams, and a commitment by Etherington to visit every single IBM location across Canada—a commitment no other IBM Canada president had ever made.

KILROY WAS HERE

The emergence of a new IBM in Canada is far from complete and many complexities remain—especially in light of the stunning $5 billion loss of IBM worldwide in 1992. The strides being made in redirecting the Canadian corporation, however, are truly extraordinary. Consider the story of Ed Kilroy. While manager of IBM's fifty-person sales branch in Vancouver, British Columbia, Kilroy saw the dramatic changes happening in the market that were proving detrimental to his branch. He became increasingly convinced, through his reading and discussions with customers and IBM agents facing similar dilemmas, that the problems (e.g., slow customer response, lack of coordination among salespeople, ineffectual decision making, limited "customer time" due to administrative requirements) were inherent in the way the structures, processes, and systems were designed. He became obsessed with developing a new, team-based organization design. In his view this would help assure greater coordination among the various functions and place decision making where it should be happening—at the point where the IBMers interface with the customer, not at someone's desk one or two levels removed. The result was a branch with essentially one level of management (Kilroy himself) and a series of teams set up to address discrete markets/customers (e.g., medical, government, small business) rather than designed around specialized functions (sales, engineering, administration, support).

While working at dramatically different levels within the IBM hierarchy, both Etherington and Kilroy were *champions for change*—and both have been highly effective. A champion is a person, or in some instances a small group of people, who introduces the change to HPWSs and then serves to support and protect the organization throughout the transition. The role is critical. The success of any transition to HPWSs is more closely tied to how effectively the champion carries out his role than any other single factor. Predictably, unsuccessful efforts typically involve a lack of effective leadership and direction. This is often demonstrated by the inability of the champion to influence upper managers and peers about the legitimacy of the effort, or by his lack of knowledge about the current state and specific needs of the organization.

A CHAMPION FOR CHANGE

A commonly held myth about HPWSs is that only those residing in the upper echelons of the organization can truly champion the change: A president or vice president can be an effective champion; a line supervisor cannot. In reality few corporate presidents lead major change efforts—and there is considerable evidence that those who do are rarely as effective as Etherington. In fact, the further removed an executive is from the day-to-day realities of an operation, the greater the likelihood that his commitment to change will sound like well-intended but poorly grounded platitudes. Most significant efforts start with champions who have never seen the executive suites and manage organizations with fewer than five hundred people. They, like Kilroy, simply know there has got to be a better way and they pursue it with tenacious commitment.

While middle- and lower-level managers can be highly effective champions, it is not a role open to just anyone—regardless of the strength of their heartfelt convictions and desires. The requirement for entry is that the potential champion manages a definable unit. For Etherington, the definable unit was IBM Canada; for Kilroy it was the Vancouver branch. For a general manager it would be the division she heads; for a front-line supervisor it would be his immediate work group. A champion is not limited by her level in the hierarchy—the limiting factor is the degree of direct control and influence she has over the systems, structures, and processes of the team she is helping to transform.

Obviously, those lower in the management hierarchy will usually have less opportunity to influence the redesign of the total system than those higher up. There are factors limiting the ability of a first-level supervisor, for example, to spread HPWSs to other parts of the organization if there is no support from senior management. The supervisor can have success in turning his own work group into a highly effective team, but as the issues the team faces go beyond their realm of control and influence (e.g., budget for equipment acquisition, access to costing data, changes to the compensation system), the resistance and general lack of support they are likely to encounter will dramatically increase. Correspondingly, the gains they are capable of achieving will slow as this resistance has a more pronounced effect on their ability to operate. The bottom line is simply: At some point in the change process it becomes clear that without higher levels of support, little future gain is likely.

THE THREE ATTRIBUTES OF A CHAMPION

In defining the attributes an effective champion must possess, the ability to *influence* is clearly among the most critical. For most organizations, the introduction of HPWSs represents a radical departure from the current, dominate management practices. Many people in the organization will have a vested interest in avoiding change, especially if the change is perceived as a possible threat to their status or prestige. The effective change champion must be able to influence people, especially higher-level managers and peers, to support the effort.

The road to becoming an effective influencer is not easy—but it's clearly necessary. While trying to establish a team-based system, Kilroy found a large percentage of his time being taken up with presentations to his manager and members of the staff. He recognized how important it was that other branch managers saw what he was doing in a positive and nonthreatening light. Gene Hendrickson, the plant manager of Tektronix's innovative circuit-board manufacturing facility, would regularly offer tours in order to get members of other key support organizations "on board with our system." The tours helped in two ways:

1. To educate other key managers about HPWSs
2. To open up the communication channels that might otherwise have been filled with speculation and rumors rather than understanding and facts

The second key attribute of champions rests in their ability to take the pulse of the organization. Champions must understand the issues, concerns, challenges, and aspirations of the people who make up the organization. They must have *contact with organization realities*. The introduction of HPWSs requires a leader who is aware of both the needs of the business and the needs of the people. Managers who distance themselves from the work force tend to invite suspicion and distrust. Conversely, managers who are regularly seen on the shop floor or out in the field and who are good listeners when someone has a comment or an idea are usually seen as being "in touch" with the real-life concerns of people. By being "in touch," these managers tend to be more trusted by the very people whose support will be so critical to the successful implementation of HPWS practices.

Like Etherington, former Steelcase CEO Frank Merlotti visited locations throughout North America. In total he met with eleven thousand employees to demonstrate his commitment to teams and his desire to listen to the real-life concerns of the company's work force. Merlotti is outspoken about the power of being in contact with the organization on this personal level and notes, "It may be no big deal to you, but it's a big deal to the team. . . . The point for senior management in listening to individual work teams is to encourage the behavior, not to sit in judgment of the results."[2]

The third attribute is having a working *knowledge* of HPWSs, including their potential risks and benefits. The means through which this knowledge is acquired differs greatly: For some it's through books, seminars, or plant tours; for others it's actual real-life experience. Regardless of how the knowledge is acquired, the change champion must have a high level of understanding of HPWS concepts and very strong convictions about their relevance to his or her organization.

At Eastman Kodak, 13 Room's Ralph Olney developed much of his knowledge relating to HPWSs during his staff study group sessions. For Gene Hendrickson it was developed through previous management experiences. In the case of Kilroy, it was a combination of books and discussions with experts. In each case, the individual who would serve as the champion for the effort had an in-depth understanding of HPWSs before he attempted to go forward. This knowledge is critical.

The ability to *influence* others by gaining their trust and acceptance; maintaining *contact* with the daily realities of the organization; and having *knowledge* of HPWSs and their organizational implications—these are the essential prerequisites for anyone taking on the role of a champion for change. It is important that a balance be maintained in all three of these arenas. Being in touch with the realities of the organization (contact) while being ineffective at gaining support and commitment (influence) from others, for example, can lead to disaster. The story of Dr. John Preston[3] amplifies this important point. It chronicles how a dedicated champion helped his team achieve a remarkable success that had dire consequences.

FIGURE 6: Leader Readiness Matrix

	Low Ability to influence leadership (clout) High	
High Contact with organization (touch)	Does not currently possess enough influence to effectively carry out the change. Focus on improving influencing/leadership capabilities. **Lacks influence**	Has the ability to effectively influence leadership and fully understands organization needs. **Change agent**
Low	Lacks a basic understanding of the organization and is ineffective at influencing the leadership. Focus on heightening awareness and influence. **Non-change agent**	Does not fully understand the current organization "realities." Focus on improving working knowledge and direct contact with the organization. **Lacks contact**

THE STORY OF A SUCCESSFUL FAILURE

Dr. John Preston felt he'd never really had the opportunity to demonstrate his talents while at Z-Technology (Z-Tech). Now, in the spring of 1987, came the Pepper Project. "Pepper" was the code name for a new product-development effort that he believed could not only get Z-Tech back into the instrument controller market, but put the company in a position to dominate it—and Preston had been the one selected to manage the project. It was a high-risk endeavor, just the kind he liked. To pull it off he knew it would take some very unconventional methods and a management style that generated unyielding commitment.

Preston's vision was to beat Z-Tech's major competitor to the market by having a new product out in just seven months. Once that was achieved, the next step would be to follow it with a series of product upgrades that would put the competition further and further behind. Ideally, these upgrades would come out every six months. The competition would suddenly find itself drowning in a sea of Z-Tech's instrument controllers. Preston's ultimate goal went even further. He was not interested in just developing a single new product or series of products; he wanted to have such an impact on the market that a new business was created. His dream was the creation of an entirely new division.

"You Have to Play for High Stakes"

Preston's vision was powerful, but few believed it was attainable. Major new product-development efforts of this complexity typically took two years; eighteen months was considered exceptional performance. Still, Preston was not deterred. The more the obstacles mounted against him, the greater he liked the challenge. He believed he could be successful if given enough freedom to operate. He even told the division general manager that if the Pepper Project was not completed on time he would resign. As Preston summarized, "If you want high performance, you have to play for high stakes."

Preston found an isolated office area half a mile from the company's headquarters. The isolation was important to him. He wanted to protect his team from the policies and practices typical within the corporation, many of which he believed greatly slowed product-development efforts. Further, he didn't want upper management looking over his shoulder. He knew what he was after was going to require a different kind of approach and mindset than most in the company were used to. He knew that much of the time the Pepper team would be operating outside the "laws" of the corporation.

The team was a talented group of hardware engineers, software engineers, and marketing professionals. Many shared Preston's perspective that product-development cycles could be dramatically reduced and had been frustrated with the bureaucracy they'd been embroiled in during the course of previous projects. Preston noted that his team was made up of professionals "who were running away from something."

The Power of the Shark

Shortly after all the members of the project team were identified, Preston, with the help of a consultant, planned an off-site meeting. The purpose of the meeting was twofold:

1. To develop agreements about how the team would work together.
2. To define the project goals.

At the session, the following principles and goals were developed:

TEAMWORK PRINCIPLES
- Shared power
- Consultative decision making
- Motivational culture
- Professional code
- Trust
- Stress expertise over status or position

GOALS
- All involved hooked into bringing it off
- Have a clean, crisp, real product introduction

In Preston's mind, the teamwork principles meant that everyone should be directly involved in all the decision making. To do this, he began holding meetings every Wednesday, during which all decisions relating to the project were made by a consensus of the entire group. Participants were allowed to speak only when they were holding a small stuffed shark (Jaws). As an individual finished speaking, he or she would put Jaws at the center of the table, and the next speaker would have to pick it up before beginning to talk. As strange as this sounds, it served the purpose of assuring that no one in the group, especially Preston, dominated conversation and thereby unfairly influenced the decision-making process. If consensus could not be reached on an issue, it was brought up at the next meeting and discussed again. When a final decision was made, the process assured that everyone on the team had complete buy-in. This inclusive approach made implementation exceptionally fast. As one team member put it, "When things were decided, we clearly understood why, and we were ready to go with it."

The Knock-Down, Drag-Out Sessions

Preston used an additional type of meeting as well—regularly scheduled "offsites." These meetings never lasted more than a day and were often just four hours in length. Offsites typically focused on planning or on interpersonal working relationships. Sometimes the interpersonal sessions turned into "knock-down, drag-out fights where we were brutally honest with one another." These meetings, though at times very difficult, served to strengthen the working relationships among team members. As one member observed, "You always came out of those sessions feeling a lot better. Everything was off everybody's chest and out in the open, where problems could be dealt with. They made us a stronger team."

Preston believed that total participation had to be the model for success. This was as evident at presentations as it was at team meetings. The first time Preston was asked to review the project before the company's vice presidents, he brought every member of the team into the conference room. Then, after some brief opening comments, he turned the presentation over to the team. According to Preston, "Everyone deserved exactly the same recognition and the same opportunity to speak—we were a team."

The "Top Gun" Work Culture

With sixty-hour work weeks common, one of Preston's primary concerns was how to keep the work environment fun and motivating. Oddly, he got a clue for how to do it from the movie *Top Gun*. Several members of the group, along with Preston, had greatly enjoyed the movie and suggested that it be the "Pepper Project's official theme." Pretty soon *Top Gun* baseball caps, movie posters, and models of F-14 fighter jets started showing up in the work area. In addition, the group members started buying Pepper dolls, Pepper T-shirts, and Pepper mugs to give away to vendors and potential customers. Interestingly, from all this a kind of hierarchy of gifts emerged that denoted the level of acceptance individuals outside the project team had among its members. This was known as the group's "terms of endearment"— taken from the title of yet another popular movie. At the lowest level T-shirts and mugs with a large cartoon of a dancing pepper were given out. At the higher levels a wind-up pepper and an F-14 model jet were given. The ultimate recognition—reserved for those making the most significant contributions to the project— was a nickname from the movie *Top Gun* (e.g., Maverick, Ice Man, Viper). As one group member explained, "The less an item cost, the higher the person had progressed on our 'terms of endearment.' It sounds silly, but I know of several instances, one in particular, where a vendor worked long and hard for us because we gave him a couple of F-14 model jets and a wind-up pepper for his kids. When he got a call sign [i.e., a nickname from *Top Gun*], he was really pleased."

The Barrier Buster

Preston was seen by group members as the architect of the emerging work culture, although he saw his role in a much simpler vein. His primary concern was to help create a motivating work environment and to remove barriers that were detrimental to achieving the seven-month time-to-market goal. He began to realize that removing barriers often meant simply encouraging people to do exactly what they thought needed to be done. Soon team members realized that they didn't always need to go through Preston to get approval—after all, you could always count on his support.

One early barrier was Z-Tech's lengthy purchasing system. The system required the purchasing department to be directly involved in all expenditures that led to acquiring pieces of equipment or component parts. Purchases of critical items were often delayed by a week or more. Team members began to purchase the parts they needed with their personal Visa cards and avoided the purchasing system altogether. As this practice increasingly raised concerns and issues in other departments, Preston vigorously defended the practice as completely necessary and scoffed at the questions raised as further evidence of how the corporate structure needlessly prolonged the development cycle.

Another barrier the group identified was the operating effectiveness of some of the support groups within Z-Tech. The group felt it would be better to farm out certain work, such as manual writing, to an outside company rather than have it done internally. Preston once again defended this approach on behalf of the team when his superiors began asking tough questions. Some began to accuse the project members of "not being team players," and acting "elitist." The criticism did not deter Preston or members of the project team. "It's people like them [senior management] that make the NPI [new-product introduction] cycle so long," insisted one team member.

Bittersweet Success

The Pepper Project did achieve its seven-month development goal, with the product entering the market over a year ahead of the competition. Preston was given the company's prestigious

Key Achievement Award for this accomplishment. An operational model of the instrument controller was put on permanent display at Z-Tech's corporate headquarters. Shortly after product introduction, however, Preston's dream of creating a new division was dissolved. He was removed from the team and assigned to a different project. A year later he resigned from Z-Tech out of frustration. One executive summarized the Pepper Project this way: "What they accomplished was remarkable, but they burned a few too many bridges in the process. If you are going to be *that different*, you must also be gracious."

THE DOWNFALL

In analyzing the case, it is clear that Preston recognized that the creation of a high performance team was the key to shortening Z-Tech's product-development cycle. His level of knowledge regarding HPWSs was fairly sophisticated—a combination of previous work experiences as well as being well read on the subject. Preston was also aware of both the frustrations and needs of team members. He worked very hard to create a "fun and motivating" work culture. The design of the team meetings and offsites assured that everyone had a voice in decisions and that interpersonal issues had a forum by which the team could address them.

While Preston was great at developing a highly effective team, he failed in managing the way Pepper interfaced with neighboring organizations. Preston's downfall was in his inability to gain the other areas' vital support. In fact, many of his tactics—ignoring the purchasing system, refusing to consider using in-company manual writers, being openly critical of other groups—served to alienate many department heads whose support would have been critical for the formation of a new division. As one Pepper team member observed, "We were good, and we were determined. Nothing was going to stop us. We had to step on some toes to get our job done, and we did not do a good enough job of managing that. We were a little too insular. People in other groups got upset." Preston himself summarized it this way: "We were naive in our group. We thought if people saw our momentum and successes we would have their support. We foolishly—arrogantly—believed that people would look the other way on some of the things we did."

For a champion to be effective at influencing, he must have a degree of political savvy and the ability to be graceful—especially with those who may disagree with his approach but whose support is vitally necessary. Preston never achieved a strong position of influence. He put little emphasis on this aspect of his role and, in the end, it contributed to the failure of his longer-term aspirations.

Taking on the role of the initiator for the transition to HPWSs is both challenging and dangerous. It requires an uncommon set of skills and presents formidable obstacles. It is as potentially rewarding as it is potentially career limiting.

The three core attributes—influence, contact, and knowledge—must be in place during the initiation of the effort and be continually enhanced throughout the entire transition. They are the essential prerequisites for starting and sustaining the effort. Failure to master a strong position of influence or to lose touch with the primary issues felt in the organization will ultimately render the champion ineffective.

CHAPTER **5**

The Essentials of Major Change

Reflecting on the highly successful transition to high performance teams at Johnsonville Foods, CEO Ralph Stayer noted, "I discovered that change occurs in fits and starts, and that while I could plan individual changes and events, I couldn't plan the whole process."[1]

BEYOND BIG CHANGE

It is easy to underestimate the magnitude and complexity involved in introducing high performance work systems. Champions of the effort, like Stayer, are attempting to navigate the organization through a complex series of changes that directly affect a variety of systems, processes, and structures. In fact, during the course of a successful implementation, virtually nothing will be left untouched. As one disgruntled manufacturing manager observed, "There is change, and then there is *big* change. Introducing high performance teams is somewhere beyond *big* change."

"Big change" seems to be spreading like an epidemic to even

America's most conservative organizations. Nobody is immune. Yesterday's premier companies, like General Motors and IBM, are experiencing the most dismal performance in their respective histories. Education reform stands as one of the most pressing social and political issues of our time. Decreased revenues and taxpayer revolt have put unprecedented pressure on federal, state, and local government to restructure to decrease costs while improving the quality of services. Organizations as diverse and as traditional as hospitals, financial institutions, and defense contractors are experiencing pressures that were unthinkable a mere decade ago. The common conclusion reached in these organizations is that the status quo is out of touch with today's realities. Major, gut-wrenching, in some cases "bet your company" change is becoming a fact of life. "The one thing we know," noted an IBM executive, "staying the same isn't an option."

THE CHANGE ESSENTIALS

It is important to recognize the distinction between more traditional approaches to change, which have tended to promote incremental improvement, and the requirements of "big" or transformational change that so many organizations are facing today. Incremental change typically does not challenge the fundamental, core elements of the organization. The culture, the commonly followed norms or rules of behavior, the existing structures and processes are not the focus of reform, they are the accepted givens. Incremental change emphasizes how to improve these various elements but does not challenge the very validity of their existence. For this reason, the implementation of high performance work systems can be traumatic. In establishing these systems, the focus is on how to alter the very heart of the beast and it clearly challenges the legitimacy of the status quo. It seeks not incremental improvement but complete trans-

FIGURE 7: Incremental vs. Transformational Change

Incremental Change	Transformational Change
• Does not challenge assumptions or values of existing culture	• Attempts to alter the culture
• Modifies and slightly improves the overall operation	• Focuses on significant, breakthrough improvements
• Uses existing structures, procedures, and processes	• Challenges the relevance of existing structures, procedures, and processes
• Minor disruption to "status quo"	• Dramatically alters the "status quo"
• Relatively low risk	• Relatively high risk

formation and creation of something fundamentally different and, it is hoped, fundamentally better.

To carry out a change of such magnitude there are a variety of conditions, or what might be referred to as *change essentials*, that greatly increase the likelihood that the effort will be successful. These essentials are the attributes most often in place during the successful implementation of high performance teams across a broad spectrum of organizations and industries. These eight change essentials serve as sound guidelines for consideration among those directly involved in either managing or serving as a resource during the transition of their organization.

1. A Strongly and Widely Felt Need for Change

Former Tektronix vice president Fred Hanson was insistent on sharing information with employees as a way to help them fully understand the current condition of the business. Surrounded by critics, Hanson believed in the simple principle that people need to be treated like business partners. As part of a large-scale training effort during the transition to high performance teams at Martin Marietta, employees were asked to present to the senior

FIGURE 8: The Change Essentials

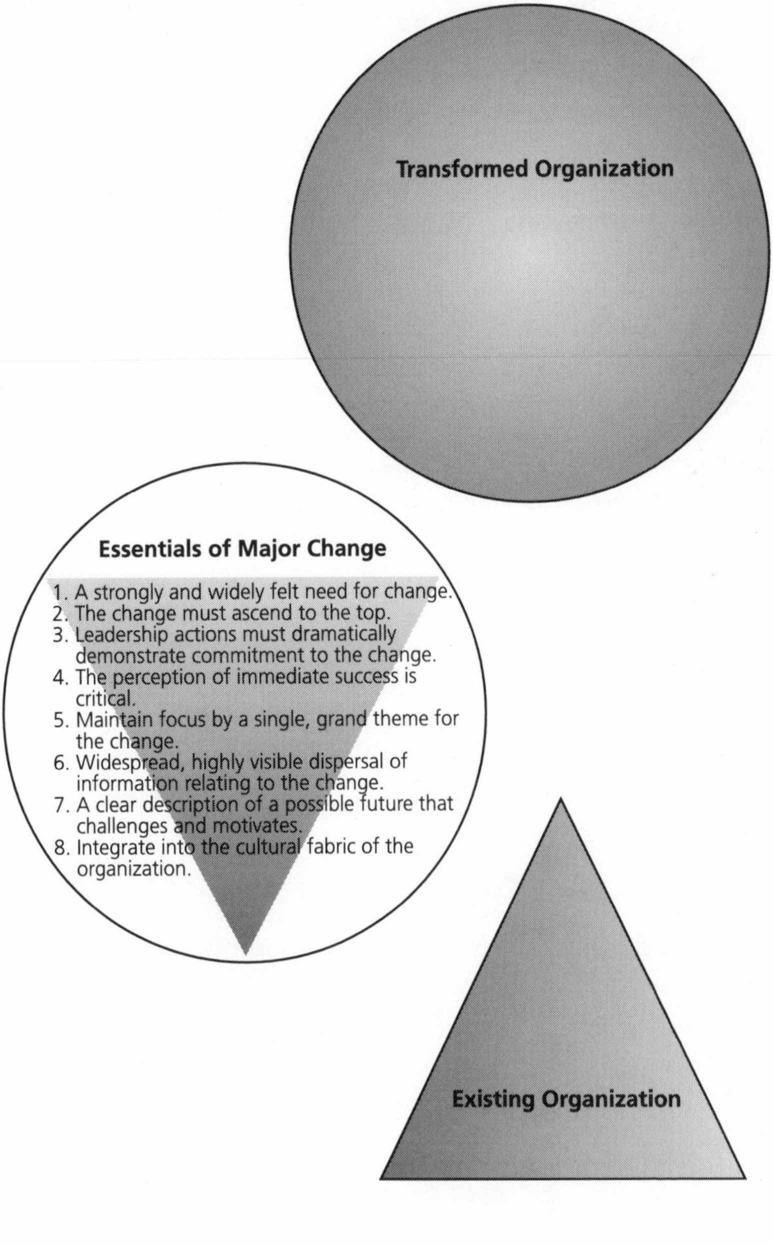

Transformed Organization

Essentials of Major Change

1. A strongly and widely felt need for change.
2. The change must ascend to the top.
3. Leadership actions must dramatically demonstrate commitment to the change.
4. The perception of immediate success is critical.
5. Maintain focus by a single, grand theme for the change.
6. Widespread, highly visible dispersal of information relating to the change.
7. A clear description of a possible future that challenges and motivates.
8. Integrate into the cultural fabric of the organization.

Existing Organization

managers of the Astronautics Group reasons why they felt the change was important. "The management team sat through perhaps a hundred presentations," noted Bill Belgard, the consultant hired by Martin Marietta to help them with the transition. "The commonality between the presentations was remarkable—it was just that never before had people been asked to think about the current condition of the business and what had to be done to keep the organization viable into the future. By the end it was crystal clear to everyone why the change needed to happen and what role high performance work teams would play."

It is obvious that without some kind of widely felt need for change it is unlikely any energy will be put toward altering the current direction of an organization. Often this felt need occurs when management realizes the company is facing a business environment that is essentially hostile to the organization's current orientation. Without significant change, management recognizes that the very survival of the company is in question. Most high performance work-team initiatives begin with this common reality—a very real challenge to the company's future.

If the case for change is not effectively communicated and clearly understood by the entire population of the organization, then the relevance of introducing high performance teams will never become clear to the very people who will be most critical to the success of the effort. Although it may seem simple, one of the most often repeated failures is management's inability to communicate why the change is important. Sometimes managers consciously refuse to discuss the rationale behind major changes with the work force. Often managers believe they are protecting people from "unnecessary and destructive worry." This was the prevailing attitude at Tektronix prior to Hanson's arrival. Management felt justified in keeping the terrible financial performance of the Portables Division confidential as a way to avoid any panic over the possibility of layoffs and as a way to help curb the possible exodus of talented people from the corporation. A paternalistic attitude often does more to frustrate employees than protect them—and without employees' support, the effort is destined to fail. Put quite simply, the greater the number of people within the organization who clearly understand the case for change, the greater the potential energy that will be generated toward achieving it.

Felt need for change does not solely emerge from the recognition of dismal performance. Admittedly, that feature has been in place among most of the major organizational change efforts that have occurred during the course of the last decade. In fact, many organizational theorists talk about the need for "pain" (e.g., the organization has lost significant market share or is losing money) to be present before most managers and employees are motivated to action. Contrary to this perspective, there are numerous examples of "healthy" organizations that have undergone significant transitions.

Boeing's Commercial Airline Division, with a $100 billion backlog that extends out over a decade and 56 percent market share is, by any business measure, healthy. Yet in two of their Washington State plants the transition to high performance teams is proceeding at an aggressive pace. Microsoft, whose utter dominance of the software industry has sent its stock skyrocketing to such heights that two thousand of its employees are now millionaires, has begun experimentation with teams in sales, product development, and manufacturing. Similarly, several claims processing groups within the highly successful Aetna insurance company are making the transition to a team-based system. What is the case for change in these organizations? At Boeing, it stems from the need to cut costs in order to maintain its enormous market share. At Microsoft, it is part of a strategy to more effectively manage growth and expansion. At Aetna, it is to provide superior service. But in none of these examples does the case for change reflect doom and destruction. All three organizations are currently experiencing extraordinary success and prosperity. The key is that the felt need for change is perceived by managers and workers alike as being relevant—even critical—to the long-term viability of the business. If the introduction of high performance work systems is divorced from the "real" business issues and seen as an effort to create a "make everybody happy" workplace, then it is unlikely to get the necessary support it needs from the stakeholders who will be most critical for its successful implementation. Even the most persuasive of leaders will have difficulty gaining followers if there is no apparent connection between the change and the eventuality of increased performance and/or competitive advantage for the organization. The reason is simple: Why take the organization through large-scale change—a long and difficult process—if there is no obvious business gain?

2. Change Ascends to the Top

Virtually anyone, given strong dedication and commitment, can influence the direction of an organization. There are numerous examples of mid-level managers and professionals who have effectively influenced leaders at the top of the management chain to support the implementation of high performance work systems. IBM Canada's Ed Kilroy served as both champion and influencer. Following his decision to use high performance teams as the means to improve the effectiveness of the Vancouver, British Columbia, sales branch, Kilroy set out to gain the support of his superiors. Being attentive to opportunities as they unfolded, Kilroy made several presentations to the sales vice president and members of his staff. Within a few months he was listed in an internal memo as being one of the company's "experts" on high performance teams. As stronger statements came out from the senior management ranks about the importance of team-based work systems, Kilroy's name, and interest in what he was doing in Vancouver, kept resurfacing. Thanks to his ability to gain upper-management support, he was given lots of latitude to experiment.

The strategy of Kilroy and other influencers is to move their ideas up through the organization. Their "realm" is in the use of clout and knowledge to elevate their perspectives up the hierarchy to where they are able to gain the necessary support to change the various systems and processes that are beyond their direct control. These systems typically include corporate policies, financial reporting and budgeting, and reward and compensation systems. Each corporate process or system can clearly stunt the transition of its organization to high performance teams. Without this far-reaching support, many changes can be easily dismissed or ignored by lower-level managers who may feel threatened by the change. Changes attempted without a high level of support will predictably be met with strong resistance.

Ironically, in large corporations many efforts at change that are initiated by the company's most senior managers fail in producing positive results. This presents an interesting contradiction. While on the one hand senior-level support is critical to success, senior managers often initiate programs that fail miserably. For top managers to be part of the solution, rather than part of the problem, they must do a good job of empowering others rather than attempting to force-feed the change themselves. An exhaustive study by Harvard Professor Michael Beer substantiates that most successful transformations start at the "periphery of the corporation in a few plants and divisions far from corporate headquarters. And," he adds, "they are led by general managers of those units, not the CEO or corporate staff people."[2]

Why do most successful efforts at change in large companies tend to begin at the periphery? These efforts are highly focused on the specific outcomes the unit needs to achieve in order to improve its performance. By contrast, corporate-driven initiatives tend to focus on abstract concepts like "participation" or "culture"—concepts that line managers have difficulty relating to in terms of bottom-line improvement.

Senior managers, who in reality have a limited role in driving the change, can have a more powerful impact by working to create a climate where HPWSs can flourish. They can accomplish this by:

1. Defining the company's direction while not insisting on specific solutions
2. Spreading the lessons learned from both successes and failures
3. Giving ongoing support and encouragement to those organizations making the transition to HPWSs
4. Reorienting corporate staff function to help support the efforts[3]

For managers trying to champion the change to high involvement at the division, plant, or even work group level, there are two simple lessons. First, work hard to gain the support of senior managers throughout the transition. If upper-management support is never gained, then there will be severe limitations on the scope and success of the change effort. Even lukewarm support by upper management may be the "kiss of death." In one instance a company president, claiming he was eager to get started with introducing high performance teams, was dumbfounded by my assessment that the 40 percent turnover rate in the manufacturing department had to be reduced before any meaningful work could even begin. "But that will cost time and money," he seemed to be saying. "I thought this was going to be an easy and quick fix." In other cases top-level executives take on a wait-and-see attitude before committing themselves to support the implementation of high performance practices even though they agree "philosophically" with the concept. Change means trauma; major change means major trauma. If top management is not willing to support the changes happening on the periphery, then there is little chance their subordinates will be supportive either. Work with them, and help them understand the benefits to the company and the specific actions they can do to help assure success.

The second lesson—don't wait for a corporate program or edict to help make the transition easier—probably won't help very much if at all. In fact, if the change to a "participative work culture" is being presented as a cure-all program by corporate, take the pieces of it that are relevant to helping improve the performance of your organization and ignore the rest. The ownership for the change must reside with the local unit that is being affected by the change and not by a corporate group that has been mandated to "change the culture."

3. Leadership Actions Dramatically Demonstrate Commitment to Change

Shortly after becoming plant manager of Weyerhaeuser's New Bern, North Carolina, facility, George Henson told his managers that he knew nothing about making pulp—that was their job. "My job," he said, "is to provide the resources you need and to protect you from the wolves." A skeptical audience, hardened by labor and contract disputes that had erupted into a seven-month-long strike, listened. Nearly a decade later—a period that had seen the remarkable transformation of the facility—a union member observed, "If George had given up in a reasonable amount of time, it wouldn't have worked. He stuck with it—even when the performance wasn't there. He was always consistent and he kept all his promises."

Champions who say the right words but whose actions do not live up to them will fail in trying to pull off a significant change. And, in a society raised on the dramatics of television (what some are beginning to call the "MTV Generation"), merely saying the right thing and doing the right thing may not be enough either. The expression I formerly used with managers was "Walk your talk," which meant always make sure your rhetoric regarding the change is wholly consistent with your daily actions. Based on what I have more recently experienced, walking your talk may not be enough, especially if the change is seen as being counter to a particular manager's personal style. In such cases the rhetoric needs to be demonstrated by *dramatic* actions. This means behaviors need to be seen that were formerly unthinkable by this leader before she began leading the change. The actions and words must almost overstate the leader's commitment. People within the organization must begin to see the champion as a "true believer"—she must begin to personify the change itself.

There are many examples of leaders who have dramatically demonstrated their commitment and through it energized others to action. One general manager who was trying to emphasize the importance of quality during his organization's transition to high performance showed up on a swing shift and started scrubbing the walls in the manufacturing area with a brush. "How can we expect quality work in all this filth?" he said. Word spread throughout the area like wildfire. Within a week the manufacturing associates and managers had completely cleaned up the entire area; a powerful point had been dramatically made. In another instance a manager, who was finally fed up with the effect of status distinctions and perks on the relationship between managers and labor, showed up at work with a baseball bat and started swinging at the sign designating his reserved parking space. In minutes, it was little more than a crumpled piece of sheet metal.

Certainly one should not glean from these examples that stubbornness, brushes, and baseball bats are the only way to demonstrate commitment. Commitment must be clearly demonstrated and widely recognized among the people in the organization whose support for the change will be critical. The questions managers need to ask themselves are: What will others say that I stand for? What is the message that they are receiving about me by the actions I regularly demonstrate? How can I profoundly demonstrate my commitment to this change?

4. The Perception of Immediate Success

Any large-scale effort to implement high performance teams is a long-term change by definition. It would be unusual (if not impossible) for a major transformation of a complex organization to take less than three to seven years. Given this fact, most experts emphasize the importance of keeping a long-term perspective and not expecting immediate results. This is a logical argument from a rational viewpoint. The pressures that exist in organizations—and the forces against change in particular—are not rational, however. I believe a key milestone must be attained quickly (within the first six months to one year). If there is not some success that can be pointed to and discussed, it is unlikely that the change will be allowed three to seven years to unfold. Success is the greatest way to combat resistance. By having an early success, more people are likely to be supportive (or at least neutral) who might have otherwise resisted the change. Attainable subgoals must be planned into the effort. In other words, the transition plan must clearly outline how an early success can be reached. Once this success is achieved, it must then be given lots of visibility. This formula, it should be added, is as true for small implementation efforts (such as a single team making the transition) as it is for large, total-organization efforts. The perception of immediate success is critical. As one general manager noted, "There's nothing like a little success to keep the skeptics at bay."

An additional point: There are lots of examples today of organizations that have introduced high performance practices and not seen any initial "performance dip"—a phenomenon once believed to be "inevitable." The commonly held belief was that as the group spends more of its regular "production" or "working time" in nonproduction activities such as training, increased information sharing, and problem-solving meetings, there must be a corresponding decline in performance. Over time this will be offset by the increased productivity and quality performance that can be attributed to the enhanced capabilities gained through these "nonproduction" activities. What has become increasingly apparent is that by predicting the performance dip, many organizations were, in fact, condemning themselves to experience it—simply, it became a self-fulfilling prophecy. The dip is not inevitable. Instead of anticipating an initial downturn, organizations should focus on how to create an early success. It is the performance climb that must be thought of as inevitable.

The success of Eastman Kodak's 13 Room exemplifies the point. During their transition to teams, this two-hundred-person group experienced no initial performance decline, just a series of continuous improvements in virtually every category they measure (quality, output, cost, up time, safety, and quality of work life). A mere two years after their effort began, one manager commented, "Our role today is so different that if a supervisor from ten or fifteen years ago were to come here and see what we're doing he'd have a stroke." The entire orientation of the organization had dramatically changed—regular team meetings, cross-training in key skills, team responsibility, accountability for decisions affecting virtually every facet of production, and two fewer levels of management. From the onset of the effort, the impressive results helped fuel support and lessen resistance.

5. A Single, Grand Theme for the Change

A former General Motors employee recalled how a manager hired a marching band to help kick off a quality program in the Pontiac Division. "You had workers standing in crankcase oil and covered in grime watching in disbelief as the band marched by. It was completely absurd and pointless. No one took the initiative seriously from that day forward."

Introducing the next big program "to finally turn things around" will predictably be met with cynicism and resistance. Most older employees have seen a variety of well-intended programs come and go like the colors of autumn. While conducting a training session at Martin Marietta, an employee came to me, sized me up, and then asked, "Is this for real or just the next program of the month?" He then went on to rattle off a long litany of programs he'd seen that, in his words, "never amounted to nothing." In a division of Rockwell, twenty-seven different initiatives were happening at once! "We began to ask ourselves," reported one manager, "how can we realistically expect anyone else in the organization to be committed to all these programs when no one on the management team can even explain half of what we've got going on now?" Most people care enough about their company that they become easily frustrated when a new program is introduced seemingly based more on the latest fad than on what is really important for the business.

The very word *program* suggests something of short duration, with a definite beginning and end. As with a program on television, if you don't like it, you can merely change the channel or start doing something else. The most successful efforts at change have a single grand theme and never refer to any aspect of the change itself as part of a program. The themes are usually simple, broad in scope, and always directly tied to improved business performance. At one high-tech company, for example, the theme was "manufacturing excellence." In working toward attaining manufacturing excellence, a variety of activities was initiated, including high-involvement management, Just-in-Time manufacturing techniques, Materials Resource Planning, and Total Quality Control. At no point, however, was the goal to implement high involvement or total quality; the goal was to attain world-class manufacturing performance. These activities were a means to improve manufacturing performance, they were not an end in themselves. In addition, by emphasizing a single theme, focus is more clearly maintained on the overriding goal.

The program mentality is a direct offshoot of the desire for quick and easy fixes to complex problems. It is relatively easy, for example, to initiate a quality-improvement program—simply hire a consultant and schedule classes. This provides the *appearance* of improvement. The difficult part is challenging and ultimately changing the systems, structures, and processes that are causing the "unquality." Addressing these problems requires changes to the very heart and soul of the organization. As a result, most change programs introduced by corporations fail to produce any tangible results. (Little wonder employees are often skeptical about the next program.)

For the champion of change this is an enlightening piece of information: The transition to high performance teams cannot be perceived as another program that may or may not last. It must be viewed as a means by which fundamental change will be made in the way the business is run. Focus on a single encompassing theme that is tied directly to improved business performance, not multiple initiatives. As Steelcase's Frank Merlotti succinctly puts it, "Don't look at it as a 'program,' that can be a big mistake. It has to become a way of life."[4]

6. Widespread, Highly Visible Dispersal of Information Relating to the Change

At the IBM sales branch office in Vancouver, communication relating to the transition to high performance teams takes on a variety of different forms. Within the office regular, state-of-the-business updates are provided by the branch manager and by subgroups working on the implementation effort. Perhaps even more important than these sessions is the way the subgroups, which are working on such volatile issues as the future structure of the organization and a team-based compensation system, communicate with the entire branch population. To provide direct communication and receive direct input, these subgroups carefully document their meetings and post the summations on an electronic bulletin board. At his or her desk, each branch employee can read the latest information from the meetings and electronically respond to the latest developments. The responses are then summarized and used as input to be considered at future subgroup meetings. In this way every member of the branch is connected, on a daily basis, with the current status of the implementation effort.

The capability for exchanging information within IBM goes

even further. People interested in high performance teams, whether they are in Hong Kong, London, or Seattle, keep apprised of the latest developments and thinking on the subject through a computer link-up—what are known within the company as "electronic conferences." This linkage helps ensure that what's learned from one effort—such as in Vancouver—is immediately shared throughout the IBM system.

While most companies don't have the technical capabilities to electronically transfer information as quickly and efficiently as IBM, the point relating to the importance of making information accessible—regardless of the means used to disperse it—remains the same. Information relating to the change must be easily accessible, for it serves the critical role of helping to gain the trust of the work force. If those impacted by the change do not trust the motivations of management, then the change will never be given the support it needs in order to succeed. Mistrust is usually cultivated by inaccurate information or the lack of it altogether. If labor relations have traditionally been poor, any perception that "management is holding back what's really going on" will tend to be seen in a negative light and will likely create all kinds of rumors and speculations that will further fuel mistrust.

The open, completely honest dispersal of information will help in developing this long-standing trust. During the transition, it is absolutely essential for management to make an up-front commitment that all progress, as well as any problems, are regularly communicated. The more candid and direct management is with information, the higher the level of trust and commitment to the change by all those involved.

7. A Clear Description of a Possible Future That Challenges and Motivates

Gene Hendrickson, the plant manager of the Tektronix circuit-board manufacturing facility, came before his entire organization and told them that they were going to become the world leader in circuit-board manufacturing. He explained that this would be accomplished by such a strong commitment to developing the skills and knowledge of people that the workplace would be seen as being more like a "university than a factory." He further stated that the only barrier that people would ever experience would be the limitations of their own abilities. No organizationally imposed barriers, such as status or management structures, would get in the way.

Naturally, the eventual success of this organization depended on the actions Hendrickson took that clearly demonstrated his commitment to this vision. He often repeated and refined what he said, but the consistency of the message never changed. Soon there were others repeating his very words and exploring the implications of his thoughts. People were drawn toward what he said and believed they could help create the kind of organization he had described.

There has been a tremendous amount written on how leaders provide direction and inspire others through a vision of some possible future. Visions are important and they can provide clarity and inspiration. In most organizations, however, visions are little more than reworded objectives—sometimes taken directly from the financial section of the business plan. Vision statements abound, often displayed in "Plexiglas tombs," where they hang like paintings in a museum awaiting the curious employee to read them. Simply, the way "visions" are developed and communicated in most organizations has little to do with either leadership or motivation—they are often boring, complex, and confusing.

What is a good vision? It must, first and foremost, provide clarity of direction. The people who make up any organization are sources of energy that can either be concentrated in a unified direction or diffused along many different paths. The less clarity there is, the greater the tendency for energy to be diffused and spread out in many different directions among many different priorities. This tendency is evident in the language people use to describe their work: "I was fighting fires again today," "Everything is a top priority," "I feel like we're just spinning our wheels." By providing clarity, energy is concentrated or channeled toward a specific end—people know what is and is not important. An effective vision is one that helps to establish this clarity.

Another feature of a good, clear vision is that people find it inspirational. "We will improve our quality by three percent" is not an inspirational statement. "We will become the number-one quality producer in the world" is. The first statement is an incremental, carefully plotted, and realistic assessment of what is likely to happen. The second is a vision of a possible future.

A third feature—and perhaps the most important—is strong support. A well-articulated vision that is not visibly supported will quickly fade. Most people look for two things when they hear a champion articulating a vision for the organization: (1) Does the leader actively demonstrate his convictions about the vision on a daily basis? And (2) will the necessary resources (e.g., people, budget, equipment) be provided? A champion may have strong convictions and a dynamic presentation, but if she will not relinquish what is perceived by members of her organization to be the necessary resources, she will simply not succeed.

Three elements need to be present when successfully communicating a vision of the future. It must:

1. Provide clarity of direction
2. Be inspiring
3. Be visibly supported with budget, resources, and time

8. Integration Into the Cultural Fabric of the Organization

In the late 1970s Tektronix aggressively implemented quality circles. At their height, there were more than two hundred regularly meeting quality circles within the company. Within three years the number of remaining quality circles was about a dozen. The experience at Tektronix was by no means unique. Many U.S.

companies that introduced these programs experienced a pattern that was strikingly similar. In virtually all the instances where these programs failed, it was because quality circles never achieved legitimacy within the dominant organization structure. As the problems that were being identified and the solutions that were being recommended became more far reaching and systemic in nature, managers easily dismissed the proposals as being "out of bounds."

Many organization change efforts begin with some kind of parallel structure that operates outside of the rules and regulations of the organization's regular power structure. Quality circles remain one of the most common examples. Employees, from a variety of different groups, attend the quality circle meetings, where they openly discuss quality-related problems and issues. Once the meetings are over, they return to their respective groups, where they must conform to the practices and policies of the dominant organization. Often the practices of the dominant power structure are inconsistent with the practices occurring in the parallel organization (in this case, the quality circle meeting). It is possible that the individual who just spent an hour providing ideas for quality improvement and problem solving might return to a group where the manager discourages the open sharing of ideas, seeing them as unnecessary distractions to getting the work done. If a parallel structure like quality circles is not given legitimacy within the dominant power structure, and if it is not fully integrated into the dominant structure to the point that group managers are responsible for its success, it will eventually die.

When the senior management team at Fisher Controls recognized that the number-one factor slowing their time-to-market was their inability to make efficient and effective decisions during the definition phase of their systems-release process, they took a dramatic step. They initiated the formation of a core team, comprised of the most talented individuals from marketing, engineering, manufacturing, and sales, and gave them

FIGURE 9: The Parallel Trap

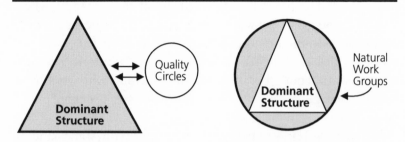

Creating a parallel structure – such as quality circles – may do little to change the practices and culture of the dominant organization.

By utilizing natural work groups, the emphasis is on fundamentally changing the way the dominant structure operates.

responsibility for managing the entire systems-release process from conception to customer delivery. According to Bob Kelly, Director of Human Resources and one of the architects of the core team design, "We had found that ad hoc task forces and quality-improvement teams simply weren't making a difference. We had tried all kinds of things and none of them really worked because we, management, often weren't acting on their ideas. We recognized the need to empower a group of people to develop a better systems-release process and truly let them, not us, be in charge of it."

The focus of high performance practices is to change the dominant power structure of the organization. As the example from Fisher Controls demonstrates, the team structure cannot be thought of as a temporary body or one that is merely making improvement suggestions. At Fisher, the core team represented a significant shift in the way a central piece of work—the systems-release process—would be completed. It challenged current organizational boundaries, existing power structures, and even the span of control that functional managers had in making decisions. The change was recognized as being so revolutionary that one senior manager confided, "This is a 'bet your company' proposition."

By contrast, parallel organizations (e.g., quality circles, steering committees, design teams) typically do very little to change this power structure, and therefore often have little lasting impact on the organization. There are, however, instances when parallel structures can prove valuable—at least on a temporary basis. Parallel structures can serve as an important catalyst to initiate the change. They help "unfreeze" the organization so that change can begin. Over time, though, the parallel structure must either become part of the new dominant power structure or, in all likelihood, its effectiveness will eventually cease. In effect, it must be sewn into the cultural fabric of the organization.

ALTERING THE CORE

The change essentials are a brief but critical list of areas for consideration when implementing HPWSs. The list is by no means exhaustive, but it does provide a good starting point when attempting to assess and plan a major change effort. There are eight essential elements. Again, they are:

1. A strongly and widely felt need for change
2. Change ascends to the top
3. Leadership actions dramatically demonstrate commitment to change
4. The perception of immediate success
5. A single, grand theme for the change
6. Widespread, highly visible dispersal of information relating to the change
7. A clear description of a possible future that challenges and motivates
8. Integration into the cultural fabric of the organization

It is the dominant structures and processes—in effect, the core of the organization—that must be changed if an effective transition to high performance systems is to succeed. The champion of the change must consistently keep this perspective in mind. Implementing HPWSs means *big change*.

CHAPTER 6

Desperately Seeking Empowerment

The forces that ultimately shape an organization are enormous and diverse. In attempting to understand how organizations change, the business press strives to simplify the complexity. What's left are the specific events (e.g., the restructuring, the turnaround, the implementation of the new technology) and the names of the senior managers associated with the efforts. These managers become the Iacoccas and Watsons of their respective organizations—the single individual whose insight and commitment led to dramatic improvement. In reality, though, they are false heroes. Rarely can the early beginnings of a major change effort be traced to the insight of the senior manager who ultimately is identified as the champion for the cause. Typically, change starts elsewhere, often somewhere in the middle, far removed from the politics of the executive offices. Only later is the cause adopted at higher levels in the company.

THE SILENT HEROES

Change initiated from the middle has had a significant impact on teaming efforts under way in companies like IBM, Shell Oil, and Corning. The champions who ultimately emerged in these

HPWS implementation efforts were the willing victims of a velvet coup—they were systematically influenced by others in the organization and eventually chose to adopt the influencers' agenda. The champions' commitment to HPWSs was molded through the efforts of others—the silent heroes of change.

THE CHANGE INFLUENCERS

Even those who are championing HPWSs within their department or group will often play a dual role: the champion for the change in their area of responsibility and the influencer for change in the areas beyond that boundary. Each role requires a fundamentally different strategy and approach. As a champion, it is important to be highly visible, to use position power to attain necessary resources, and, when necessary, to serve as a shield to protect the organization from outside pressures that run counter to HPWSs. Being an influencer requires working behind the scenes, avoiding the constraints of the formal hierarchy, and taking advantage of "chance" encounters to move ideas forward.

Influencing the direction of the organization is a role that many unlikely candidates play. They include:

1. People with limited hierarchical power
2. Mid- to lower-level managers or staff
3. People who work behind the scenes with enormous energy and dedication, striving to get their ideas heard and supported by those higher in the management chain

Influencers who are effective in getting support for HPWSs share four characteristics:

Knowledge

In general, managers are intolerant of misinformation, flowery claims, or abstract ideas. They want clear and concise facts. If the influencer is going to be taken seriously, she needs a sophisticated knowledge of HPWSs and the ability to answer the inevitably tough questions. It is especially important to be able to describe in specific (as opposed to conceptual or general) terms how similar industries have utilized team-based work systems, what their results have been, and how they structured their organizations.

Conviction

Managers are not going to take someone seriously who has not clearly defined his own convictions or who lacks visible enthusiasm for the change. The influencer must be able to describe the benefits of the effort and why he personally wants to see the organization introduce HPWSs. A strong set of personal convictions can go a long way in shaping the convictions of others—especially if the manager senses the strength and deep-down certainty of the position the influencer holds.

Risk

Managers recognize that they "never hear it the way it really is." Subordinates know it is rarely, if ever, in their best interest to bring bad news to the boss. As a result, bad news is filtered and purified. All the nastiness and foul taste is cleanly extracted before the news is passed upward. This purification process is particularly strong in organizations where there is the perception that previous messengers "have been shot." A human-resources manager at a major truck manufacturing company admitted that he systematically omitted certain information from his presentations to the company's chairman. "I retire in 2007 and I want to stick around till then. Here it's better to keep a real low profile and not rock the boat."

The perspective of this HR manager is indicative of the massive *fear of risk* that is rampant in organizations. Influencers must be able to operate at a level beyond it or they will ultimately prove ineffective. If concerns about career dictate what they are willing to say, the influencers, too, may become little more than pawns in the ongoing *purification conspiracy*. By contrast, if the influencers are beyond the fear of risk, the greatest source of influencing strength comes from their ability to provide unfiltered information and, in the words of a highly effective influencer, "tell them the things their best friend can't." The objective is for the influencer to make it okay to relate "the good, the bad, and the ugly" to the manager she is hoping will eventually champion the transition to HPWSs. Most managers respect and value someone in their organization who cuts through the bleached-out words and gets down to the raw facts.

Respect

Obviously, managers will place more significance on the ideas that come from someone whom they respect. Being well respected in the organization gives the change influencer credibility even before he speaks a word. Credibility is the essential ingredient in gaining access to, and getting a good hearing from, the key managers who can serve as champions for the effort.

The elements of knowledge, conviction, risk, and respect are the foundation on which the influencer's ability to get her case heard "on high" depends. The effectiveness of the influencer will be affected by the degree to which she embellishes these characteristics. Much of the influencer's ability to effect change is dependent on how well she is received by the managers with the legitimate authority to initiate changes in the organization. If the potential champion doubts the influencer's credibility or perceives that she is merely out for political gain, then he will quickly dismiss her recommendations. In assessing whether to take the advice seriously, he must be convinced that the influencer has provided him with enough information to address the multitude of questions firing through his mind. The potential champion will have questions like:

- Where did she develop her knowledge about HPWSs? Who else in our industry is doing it and what have been their results?
- Are her perspectives on HPWSs realistic? Can the claims that she suggests have occurred elsewhere realistically happen here given the unique qualities of the organization?
- Nothing ever happens without some cost. Has she given me a realistic assessment of the costs as well as the benefits?
- Why are her convictions on this issue so strong? What are the real underlying reasons she thinks the organization needs to move in this direction?
- What is she willing to risk in attempting to pull off this effort? What am I willing to risk?
- Do I trust and respect her? Should these comments be taken seriously given my past experiences with her and her reputation within the organization?

THE ART OF INFLUENCING CHANGE

The goal of the influencer is twofold:

1. To get HPWSs into the agendas and discussions of potential change champions
2. To make sure, to the greatest extent possible, that there is movement in the organization toward HPWSs

FIGURE 10: Characteristics of the Change Influencer

- Knowledge of HPWSs and can clearly see how they would benefit the organization (knowledge)

- A strong set of convictions as to why the organization must change its current orientation (conviction)

- Willingness to take risks—both personally and professionally—to get his ideas heard (risk)

- Highly respected in the organization for his knowledge, integrity, and honesty (respect)

The influencers' strategy is a direct reflection of their desire to meet these goals. While their work may be invisible to most in the organization, it nevertheless can play a critical role in influencing and preparing the leadership for the challenges of managing the transition to HPWSs.

Ultimately, the "buck stops" with the person in power. It would be unrealistic to suggest that change influencers can have an effect if those at the top of the organization refuse to listen to or accept their ideas. It is equally unrealistic to suggest that top-level managers will never listen to or act upon the ideas brought to them by mid-level managers and staff. Unfortunately, it is often the perception of those in the middle that they "have their hands tied"—what they say cannot make a difference. A recent survey found that only 35 percent of mid-managers felt senior management listened to their issues and ideas.[1] In reality, their ideas can, and often do, have a dramatic impact. In fact, it is fair to say that mid-managers are responsible for initiating most of the innovation that occurs in organizations.

The means for influencing change is difficult to characterize since it is not a sequential path. To the outside observer it appears like a series of loosely coupled activities that have little strategic or systematic orientation.[2] Specific actions might include:

- "Chance" conversations in the parking lot or local coffee shop with key managers
- Establishing informal networks of people interested in HPWSs
- Sending out books and articles on the subject of HPWSs to targeted individuals
- Setting up panel discussions and workshops on HPWSs
- Establishing "electronic bulletin boards" to discuss issues relating to HPWSs
- Getting on the agenda of staff meetings to discuss the potential of HPWSs
- One-on-one coaching and idea sharing with targeted individuals

While by outward appearances influencers might seem to be randomly thrashing about as they attempt to get their ideas heard, there is a method to the seeming madness. Influencers focus their energy on activities that help increase their influencing capability. These activities fall into three distinct areas:

- The creation of a vision that portrays the potential of HPWSs in the organization (new-reality creation)
- The creation of opportunities, as well as the reactions to situations as they arise, that help in gaining support for HPWSs among potential champions and key opinion leaders within the organization (leveraging serendipity)
- The ongoing demonstration of support for HPWSs even in the face of significant setbacks and strengthening resistance (bulldogged stick-to-itiveness)

NEW-REALITY CREATION

During his 1968 presidential campaign, Robert Kennedy stated, "Some people see things as they are and say 'Why?' I dream things that never were and say 'Why not?'" Kennedy's quote captures the essence of a vision—it is a statement of the organizational

FIGURE 11: Strategy for Influencing Change

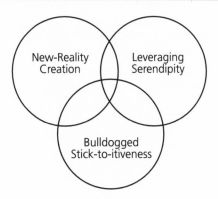

dream. It stretches the imagination and motivates. It helps us rethink what is possible and what a new, better reality could look like.

For the influencer seeking to gain support for HPWSs, creating a vivid picture of a team-based organization is a key step in gaining the support of others. Focusing on "Why not?" helps develop new possibilities:

- Why not have an organization where every employee feels like a business partner?
- Why not share information, responsibility, and authority so that all employees have a direct say in issues that directly affect them?
- Why not work in an atmosphere characterized by respect, harmony, and coordination between management and labor?
- Why not seek out levels of improvement that were previously thought unattainable?

Focusing on "Why?" may be interpreted as trying to place blame on others in order to gain politically—a position that will tend to be negatively viewed. For instance:

- Why are labor/management relations so poor?
- Why is it that we never work as a team?
- Why are people so afraid of taking on new responsibilities?
- Why is our rate of improvement so low?

As one influencer said in the opening remarks of her presentation to a senior management staff, "Let's free ourselves for a moment and not be confined by what is. What I want to discuss is what could be."

Seeing a need for a dramatic change within the company, a loose network of interested managers and professionals at Tektronix began to meet to discuss how to "transform" the company into a high performance system. The group initiated a project to create a *visioning tool*; the intent of its design was to help people throughout the organization, particularly those in senior management, better understand the characteristics of HPWSs and the potential benefits to the corporation.

The result was the creation of the "High Performance/High Commitment System Assessment Guide." In it the authors described several examples of what low performance/low commitment and high performance/high commitment organizations would look like in terms that described specific behaviors one might observe. For example, they described the range of skills that would be seen, the kinds of issues people would talk about, and the way leadership would be practiced. The intent of highlighting the characteristics of both the "low" and "high" organizations was to better illustrate the striking gap in both performance and potential. The guide became increasingly popular within the organization. Managers who, by their own admission, "knew absolutely nothing about high performance systems" found the guide useful in broadening their understanding.

A description of a possible future that inspires others is the influencer's most powerful tool in gaining the support of key figures in the organization. But it also represents a formidable challenge, as visions are not easily articulated. It is critical that the new reality be clear, concise, easily understandable, memorable, exciting, and—perhaps most important—tied directly to the business issues facing the company. The vision described by the influencer must offer a tangible way to deal with current and future demands.

LEVERAGING SERENDIPITY

The senior management team of a $200 million division was meeting to discuss product-development priorities for the coming year. Following a long morning of debate, the team broke for lunch. The general manager decided to use the break as an opportunity to visit a nearby hotel where the sales force was having its annual meeting. As the facilitator for the meeting, I established our reconvening time, reviewed the morning notes, and then sat down to a platter of cold cuts and salad with the four remaining staff members. "The meeting is going well," commented the engineering manager. "I feel like we've done a good job of assessing the market and our engineering capability."

Indeed they had. The morning had been filled with detailed presentations by personnel from marketing and engineering describing the market potential for several different product configurations and their technical feasibility. It was apparent that the group was very near a consensus.

Upon returning to the meeting room, the general manager looked pleased; he was almost beaming. "I got talking to one of the sales reps over lunch and he said we've got it all wrong," he told us. "We're looking at the wrong market entirely. I agree. Here's what we discussed. . . ." He had the enthusiasm of a child opening birthday gifts as he described the details and then proposed an entirely new direction for the product-development effort. As he finished, the marketing manager noted, "But that would be entirely different than anything we discussed this morning. Where are the facts? Where is the rationale? Why would we want to do this?"

Many decisions are based on influence and timing, not rationale and logic. Rightly or wrongly, the general manager had put more credence on a thirty-minute lunch conversation then he put in hours of detailed presentations, discussions, and debate with his entire staff. Although this example is extreme, the fact remains that many decisions that have a direct impact on corporate direction are the result of chance encounters. Influencers recognize this and attempt to leverage serendipity to their advantage.

Influencers leverage serendipity in two important ways:

1. They utilize *opportunity scripting* whereby they carefully plan out projects and meetings, and form networks and events that help them get their case heard.

2. They take advantage of *chance encounters* with key executives—
whether they occur in the lunchroom, the grocery store, or the
parking lot—by having a well-rehearsed message that outlines
their HPWS convictions.

Opportunity Scripting

Within IBM's Programming Systems Lab in Toronto, Ontario,
internal consultant Allen Class was both encouraged and frustrated. The effort to introduce HPWSs into the lab had seen some
extraordinary successes. Some of the areas making the transition
had demonstrated improvements in productivity, high levels of
commitment to team goals, and reduced inter-departmental conflict. Yet the majority of the organization remained unaffected
by the changes. They were still operating under the same old
rules, procedures, and structures. Since most of the functions
within the lab had unique product mandates, there were few
opportunities to share experiences between groups. Conse-
quently some functions viewed the team initiatives with either
curiosity or skepticism.

Class's solution was to create an event that would help the rest
of the lab understand more about HPWSs. Ideally, it would serve
the dual purpose of increasing the acceptance of the HPWSs
within the lab while being a catalyst to encourage more activity
among the "wait and see" groups. A format was needed that
provided an honest assessment of HPWSs. It also needed to be
energetic and fun. "What about a talk show, with you as Ger-
aldo?" suggested a colleague.

The idea stuck. Class got the management support he needed to
pull off the session and then went on a talk-show-watching binge.
The final format would be true to what he had seen on TV. Guests
included an expert (an outside consultant who specialized in
HPWS efforts) and a panel (employees from the areas in the lab
where teams had been successfully implemented). He would run
around with a microphone like Phil Donahue, allowing audience

members to ask questions of the guests. He would follow up their questions with probing—and even controversial—questions of his own.

The "talk show" was well received. It proved to be an effective, nonthreatening way to gain momentum and support for the HPWS effort.

While Class's influence in the lab's transition has been significant, he has limited hierarchical power. His "official" role within the organization is Manager of Team Effectiveness. Class's ability to influence the direction of the lab toward HPWSs demonstrates the impact that effective opportunity scripting can have. As one manager stated, "I think just about everyone would agree that we wouldn't be seeing the positive results we're seeing today without Allen [Class]."

Close Encounters of the Chance Kind

Chance encounters can have an impact as powerful as opportunity scripting. In fact, the majority of a manager's time is spent in both receiving and giving information in settings outside of meetings or reports. Rather than working toward their objectives exclusively through planned agendas and carefully orchestrated meetings, most managers take advantage of chance encounters to work toward their goals. Like change influencers, they take advantage of even unplanned encounters to move the organization forward.

Effective change influencers have working agendas that they carry around in their heads. When likely opportunities present themselves, they are quick to act and take advantage of them. They intuitively recognize that they often make a more powerful impression on key managers during unplanned opportunities than they do during carefully orchestrated events. If an executive happens to initiate a conversation in the lunchroom, parking lot, or even the local tavern, this might provide the perfect time to introduce a summary of HPWSs and how they could benefit the organization. These unplanned, chance encounters are one of the reasons that the pathway to influencing change is so crooked and difficult to describe. The precision and rationale for these various, seemingly unrelated activities are integrated by the internal working agenda of the change influencer. Each encounter moves the influencer closer to achieving her goal.

An influencer at Sequent Computer wandered around the executive offices on a weekly basis hoping for a "chance" encounter. An influencer at Corning carefully timed her departure from work to coincide with that of a key executive. Another influencer insisted that his desk be located in the same office complex as the group vice president. "I want him to walk by me every day so that he eventually has to ask me what's going on with my team."

While these strategies may seem contrived, it remains true that positions on many core organizational issues—including the applicability of HPWSs—are determined outside of formal meetings and strategy sessions. By leveraging serendipity, the change influencer is increasing the likelihood that his position will be, at the very least, heard and, at the very best, adopted.

BULLDOGGED STICK-TO-ITIVENESS

With the clouds of conflict darkening across Europe just prior to the beginning of World War II, Winston Churchill allegedly asked a German general if he knew why the British bulldog had a pugged nose. Taking the bait, the general responded that he had no idea. "It's so he can still breathe without letting go," Churchill explained, making it clear that the double meaning in relation to the current world events was intended.

Change influencers behave with the same heartfelt tenacity as the British bulldog—they simply don't let go. Since the legitimate, hierarchical power does not reside with the influencers, they must accept the fact that their ideas and initiatives are often going to be ignored or sidestepped. They may even come to feel that they are walking into the same wall time after time after time.

The key is their relentless desire, commitment, and simple "bull-doggedness" to keep at it even when their efforts seem to be going nowhere.

By behaving with this strong sense of tenacity, influencers display their commitment to the new realities they are advocating. This does not mean that influencers jump up on soapboxes or pound on desks—being effective also means being politically astute. Antics that would alienate the very managers the influencer is attempting to convert into champions are vigorously avoided. Rather, influencers operate with *calculated audacity*, taking full advantage of the opportunities that present themselves while politely sidestepping events that might block the implementation of HPWSs. When obstacles appear, the influencer immediately searches for new paths to achieve his desired ends. The pathway to influencing organization change is crooked and often unpredictable. The influencer must maneuver like a mountain goat, surefooted while changing directions, able to quickly find alternative routes, virtually unaffected by rises and falls.

The stick-to-itiveness demonstrated by change influencers reaches extraordinary proportions at times. Rockwell's Bill Horton, a training director in the Defense Electronics Division, made the brash decision to allocate all of his training budget to implementing HPWSs, even though he had little support from senior management. As a first step he formed a network of managers who were interested in finding out more about HPWSs. As the support grew within the network, he started a series of training sessions across the organization that provided an overview of HPWSs and developed team skills in areas like meeting effectiveness, decision making, problem solving, and action planning. The general manager, upon hearing about the activities in the organization, asked Horton if he could attend a training session. Horton gladly accommodated him. The general manager was so impressed by what he saw that he immediately gave his full support to the effort.

Just at the point where it looked as if the division was going to aggressively pursue HPWSs, defense cuts associated with the end of the Cold War suddenly put layoffs on the immediate horizon. Morale within the organization dropped and frustration grew. When the downsizing hit, it was dramatic: Entire teams were dissolved, a number of managers from Horton's original HPWS network either left or were laid off, some even began questioning the long-term viability of the entire division—was it really necessary in a post–Cold War world? Horton himself began wondering if a pink slip would soon appear on his desk.

After the flood of cuts was over, Horton surveyed what was left of the organization and started where he had temporarily left off. He reenergized the network meetings, focusing attendees' attention on how they could serve as resources to the organization as part of a master strategy to resurrect HPWSs. A new training plan to address the specific needs of the remaining teams was developed. Finally, Horton worked with the general manager and described ways in which the GM could help revitalize the effort despite the dismal climate within the organization.

There is a kind of tenacity among effective influencers—they refuse to give in or be deterred, even in the face of overwhelming circumstances. As has been the case with Rockwell's Horton, their sense of commitment often serves to inspire others to take action. Eventually their stick-to-itiveness gets recognized and their ideas get a fair hearing.

DESPERATELY SEEKING EMPOWERMENT

The cry heard from many managers and professional staff is often one of frustration: "If only senior management would get on board and support this, then things could finally improve." This perspective is disempowering—it assumes that progress can occur only if *someone else* takes action. In reality, the point where action can be taken to effect change is not dictated by one's position in the hierarchy—it is dictated by energy and willingness. Influencing change means effectively demonstrating four qualities—knowledge, conviction, risk, and respect—while pursuing a strategy of creating a vision of a possible new reality; leveraging serendipity to get the possible future heard by potential champions; and demonstrating a bulldogged stubbornness to pursue this vision even in the face of dramatic resistance. For those desperately seeking empowerment, the role of influencer is an open position.

CHAPTER 7

The Dilemma in the Middle

Mid-level managers have become the endangered species of the 1990s. Companies everywhere are scrambling to reduce their ranks, and the impact has been dramatic. From 1989 to 1991, 17 percent of layoffs have come from middle management (defined as everyone between first-line supervisors and senior management) even though they account for less than 8 percent of the total work force.[1] Little wonder many find it difficult to embrace high performance work systems, which are often touted as a way to "flatten" the organization. To make matters worse, many of the results of successful transitions seem to confirm the worst fears of managers and supervisors. At Monsanto's Greenwood plant the number of salaried managers has shrunk by 50 percent since high performance work teams were introduced. During its transition to HPWSs, Southwest Industries flattened its overall organization from seven to four levels of management.[2] Northern Telecom saw 25 percent of its first-line supervisors leave after teams were adopted at one of its facilities. Whether you look at IBM or Weyerhaeuser, the story appears the same—at sites where HPWSs have been successfully implemented, fewer managers seem to be needed than in their traditionally designed counterparts. A recent survey by *Industry Week* found that 68 percent of the companies that had work teams in place discovered they needed less supervision.[3]

THE PLANNED OBSOLESCENCE STRATEGY

A kind of hysteria has been created among many managers who are understandably concerned about their jobs. The scenario they fear most is straightforward: As teams take on more and more responsibility, the role of managers becomes increasingly diminished and ultimately redundant. While the team develops its capability to handle the various administrative, technical, customer, and decision-making responsibilities that formerly required a manager's attention, the manager's role becomes obsolete. In the end, managers become victims of planned obsolescence—and once their skill set is no longer necessary, a quick move by the company to lay off their ranks saves enormous salary and benefit costs.

Many companies have played out this scenario and aggressively pursued restructuring to teams with the singular goal of reducing "white-collar headcount." Virtually without exception, these efforts have failed miserably. In fact, the statistics bear out that downsizing is a completely flawed strategy for improving organization performance over the long run. *Nearly 80 percent of senior managers representing over a thousand corporations admitted that their restructuring efforts had failed to improve return on investment to any appreciable degree, while fully 58 percent felt that employee morale had been completely battered by the effort.*[4] There are four reasons the planned obsolescence strategy doesn't work:

1. Middle management, the targeted group for downsizing, is the group whose support for the effective implementation of HPWSs is the most critical. Few managers will knowingly strive to develop the capabilities of their team if their reward is a pink slip.

2. The amount of technical and business expertise in the middle-management ranks is often grossly underestimated. Only after they are gone are their unique contributions fully appreciated and missed. In many cases the result is to hire pricey outside consultants to fill the knowledge void.

3. Fundamentally, the planned-obsolescence strategy is based on a zero-gain proposition. Although the team is executing the manager's former responsibilities, the organization gains nothing in terms of enhanced knowledge or strategic capability by changing who carries out the role. In fact, *by laying off middle managers, significant capacity for enhancing the organization's longer-term competitive position* (in areas such as strategic planning, exploration of new technologies, developing closer ties with customers, or more effective market analysis) *is lost to the short-term cost savings of decreasing the payroll.*

4. The impact on morale and the disruption to working relationships caused by downsizing often lead to dramatic reductions in productivity and service. Many of the organization's most talented individuals—feeling the company is no longer on stable ground—leave to join other firms. These factors, which have a significant effect on the bottom line, are never calculated into the cost-savings projections that get reported to Wall Street.

PAINLESS FLATTENING

If downsizing is such a flawed strategy for increasing performance, why do so many companies that have had successful HPWS efforts report that they now have fewer managers and fewer levels of management? The answer: The reported reductions in the management ranks typically have little to do with downsizing, and everything to do with role expansion. There may be fewer individuals with the official title "manager," but far more individuals are making significant contributions to the business through their work on project teams, task forces, and development groups. So while the management ranks have decreased, the areas for individual contribution have correspondingly increased. As one manager put it, "Before I was completely absorbed in fighting fires and getting through the day as if I were in a battle. No strategy, no long-term thinking, no chance to contribute to the bigger picture. Now [since the introduction of HPWSs] that's all changed."

In the case of most successful HPWS efforts, decreases in the management ranks are an outcome of improved organization performance and not the means by which the performance improvement was gained. This distinction is important. If a massive downsizing effort is initiated as part of a strategy to create a team-based organization, the first step down the path of disaster has been taken. But if an evolutionary perspective is maintained, recognizing the tremendous value that mid-level managers can add to the development of the HPWS, then changes to structures and roles can evolve in a relatively nonthreatening manner. There are three strategies commonly used to maintain the trust and support of middle management while correspondingly helping the organization remain trim and free from excess hierarchy and bureaucracy.

1. Enhanced Performance Strategy

The intent is for managers—whose direct management responsibilities may not be necessary in the future—to enhance their contribution to the organization by taking on a new role. A powerful two-part question to help managers recognize how they could increase their value to the company begins:

1. How do you currently spend the majority of your time? (Invariably, answers include "fire fighting," "coordinating activities," "administration," "dealing with personnel issues," even "babysitting.")

The second question is the zinger:

2. If the group you currently manage could absorb all the day-to-

day activities that currently consume your time and energy, what kinds of contributions would this free you up to make to the business? (The answer to this question is nearly always filled with forward-looking ideas: "evaluating new technology," "longer-term strategic planning," "competitive analysis," "closer ties with vendors and customers.")

When managers recognize—and believe—that by enhancing the capabilities of their team they are correspondingly expanding their own opportunities to contribute to the organization, a powerful win-win dynamic is created. Increasing team effectiveness is no longer a threat to their role, but rather the means by which they can expand their own responsibilities. When played out effectively, the enhanced-performance strategy leads to fewer individuals managing people and more project teams and task forces addressing issues of critical importance to the organization.

2. Natural Attrition Strategy

One of the least utilized methods for downsizing has been to effectively manage natural attrition (e.g., retirement, people choosing to leave the company). Since the people who are leaving the firm are doing so by their own personal choice, the trauma and upheaval associated with layoffs are completely avoided. With turnover rates in the 8 to 10 percent range common at most companies, a year-long hiring freeze can go a long way toward painlessly flattening the organization.

At Southwest Industries a commitment was made to supervisors that they would not lose their jobs as employee involvement was phased in. As the teams became increasingly effective, and it became clear that the organization could operate with less supervision, natural attrition was used to reduce the supervisory ranks. Effectively managing attrition was seen as being one of the critical factors that minimized supervisor resistance to high performance teams.[5]

Another factor leading to natural attrition is the *de-selection phe-nomenon* that often accompanies the transition to HPWSs. Once exposed to HPWS concepts, some managers will recognize that the new requirements expected of them are not consistent with the way they like to operate. Many of these managers (usually somewhere between 5 and 15 percent) will choose to leave the organization to pursue opportunities in a workplace that is more conducive to their personal style. Simply by not replacing these departing managers, the organization becomes further flattened.

3. Rebuilding Strategy

It would be naive to suggest that rapid downsizing is never necessary—although it is fair to say that it is often used recklessly and inappropriately. Conditions, however, may necessitate rapid and dramatic cuts in the face of threats to the viability of the business. Such conditions faced IBM in 1991 when it experienced the first loss in its long and illustrious history. IBM, recognizing the need for large cuts to staff while wanting to maintain the trust and integrity of its "full employment" philosophy, introduced eighty-seven early-retirement and voluntary buy-out programs in thirty-seven countries.[6]

While many Wall Street analysts were critical of the move—they wanted to see immediate and massive layoffs to rejuvenate the company's financial picture—it did help IBM successfully reduce their work force by nearly 25 percent (almost eighty-five thousand employees) without any layoffs. And while it can be argued that some talented people were lost in the process—an unavoidable consequence of corporate instability—morale throughout much of IBM was maintained at a remarkably high level. Even more significant, the emergence of HPWSs at most locales came after the downsizing was complete. At these sites the introduction of HPWSs was viewed as part of a rebuilding strat-egy to create a new and improved organization.

There are two important lessons from the IBM example: First, even in instances where rapid cuts in the work force are inevitable, there are many options besides layoffs to achieve the reductions. (IBM actually studied the matter extensively and determined that its method of early retirement and voluntary buy-outs "costs no more in the aggregate than layoffs at comparable companies."[7]) The second lesson: It is important to clearly separate the need for downsizing from the transition to HPWSs. If employees, mid-managers in particular, come to think of the downsizing as being necessitated by HPWSs, then they will understandably be reluctant to support the transition.

The point is important: *If downsizing is inevitable due to current business conditions, complete the downsizing before introducing HPWS concepts to the organization.* After the downsizing is complete, use the transition to HPWSs as part of an overall strategy to *rebuild* the organization.

Despite the best intended efforts, many managers will remain skeptical and outwardly resist the transition to HPWSs. This creates the central challenge for this phase of the effort: How do you get and maintain management support while recognizing that most managers will view the transition—at least initially—as a threat? To effectively answer this question, we must first explore the two primary sources of management resistance.

THE ANATOMY OF RESISTANCE

The source of mid-level management resistance comes from two seemingly contradictory fears:

1. *The fear of role contraction.* This is the fear of losing everything the manager currently has (e.g., status, position, perks, salary, benefits, authority).
2. *The fear of role expansion.* This is the fear of not having the skills, competencies, and knowledge to be successful in the new team-based workplace.

While these sources of resistance are diametrically opposed, the way the resistance is played out in the workplace is strikingly similar. In both cases managers will be openly skeptical of HPWSs or actively work to discredit the effort; they may stunt the development of their team or even abdicate responsibility by withdrawing from team meetings and direct interactions with team members. The intended outcome of their resistance is the same: Keep things as they are.

FEAR OF CONTRACTION

The most obvious source of resistance is generated by the threat HPWSs pose to the role that managers currently perform. Managers recognize that HPWSs will require a dramatic change in how they operate and could ultimately mean a loss of status, perks, control, and—in the extreme—even employment. To further heighten frustration, the first exposure that many managers have to HPWSs stresses what they *should not* be doing. The list reads like the Ten Commandments of Management No-Nos:

1. Thou shall not make decisions for the team.
2. Thou shall not keep information from the team.
3. Thou shall not make hiring and firing decisions without team involvement and approval.
4. Thou shall not decide work assignments and scheduling.
5. Thou shall not tell team members what to do or when to do it.
6. Thou shall not solve problems for the team.
7. Thou shall not give an opinion unless asked to do so.
8. Thou shall not control, manipulate, or dictate to team members in any manner or form.
9. Thou shall not take any credit for any team achievements.
10. Thou shall not commit any action that remotely resembles the traditional management role.

This emphasis on what the role is *not* often leaves managers with the feeling that their realm of responsibility is in a cycle of continuous contraction. In the end they will become a lesser member of the team, completely stripped of their status, position, and control. Fearing this contraction, many begin resisting the transition to HPWSs for reasons of self-preservation—it is their last stand against what they perceive as the oncoming vacuum of powerlessness.

Loss of Status: The Decline of Position

The importance of position and status for many managers is often underestimated. For some it literally becomes part of how they assess their own self-worth. A manager at a Monsanto plant in Ruabon, North Wales, remarked how he liked being a manager, not because of the work or even his salary, but because of the status it gave him within the community. "I like walking down the street knowing that people see me as successful. . . . I take great personal satisfaction in telling people my position and title." To him becoming a "team leader" or a "facilitator," or being put on a "special project," was a clear loss of the status he felt he had worked so hard to achieve. "Intellectually, I understand this [HPWSs] is the right approach, but what is it that I will tell people I do?" He clearly felt the other titles carried less importance and therefore would be interpreted as an indication that his position within the company had lessened.

Loss of Perks: The Moose Tuft

Other rampant forms of status distinction include perks that are exclusive to management. It is not unusual for such things as office size, location, the type of desk allowed—even the artwork that is used to decorate the office—to be connected with a person's level in the hierarchy. An intern at a major corporation described to me the shock he felt when he found a crew tearing out the plush red carpet in his newly assigned office and replacing it with an indoor/outdoor variety dark blue in color. It was later explained to him that his low position necessitated the change in carpeting—plush red was reserved for those at the director level and above. In an even more outrageous example, managers promoted into the senior ranks of one major petroleum producer were secretly given a moose tuft—that's right, a clump of hair from the chin of a moose! Getting the moose tuft designated that you had been accepted as a member of the "inner circle."

Perks are often difficult to disband because they are seen as an entitlement by those who have received them. Many managers vigorously defend their perks as a "right they have earned" by pulling themselves up through the ranks. The reserved parking place or the executive dining room, this rationalization goes, is the result of being recognized for superior performance. In effect, the cream rises to the top, and those at the top deserve extra recognition, status, position, and benefits. What this argument misses is the damaging effect perks have on the morale of those who don't get them. Perks run completely counter to creating a culture of participation and empowerment by creating status distinctions that have no relevance to attaining business results.

Loss of Control: The Myth of Team Accountability

The apparent loss of control over the actions of the team is another difficult pill for managers to swallow—especially when the manager recognizes that she will, in all likelihood, still be held accountable for the team's overall performance. "It's not fair to be held accountable for results when you have no authority to execute actions," stated one frustrated manager. "And team accountability never works because when things break down, everyone just starts pointing fingers."

It is clearly a myth that team accountability doesn't work. Rather than the manager setting expectations and holding team members accountable for action, the entire team holds each other accountable. When effectively utilized, mutual accountability creates tremendous peer pressure to perform. In some cases managers actually find themselves trying to get the team to "lighten up" on its members—peers, they discover, are typically less tolerant of missed commitments than managers are. At an A. E. Staley plant where HPWSs were aggressively pursued in the early Eighties, peer pressure reached such an extreme level that members who didn't live up to team expectations would find their lunch pails on the stairway just outside the main entrance. The intended message was simple and clear: You didn't perform, so don't bother to come back.

For those who have never actually experienced the power of team-centered control, it is difficult to accept as being as effective as manager-centered control. Many managers look at people in their group, do a mental assessment of their potential, and are convinced that HPWSs simply won't work. The comments are predictable: "No one in my group wants to take additional responsibility" and "People are happy right where they are now." In a sense, these managers are right—as long as their current set of management practices remains, people probably will not accept extra responsibility and probably can't be expected to make good decisions. It is a self-fulfilling prophecy: If the manager fundamentally believes that her group can't act in a responsible manner, she will never give them the opportunity to demonstrate otherwise. Ultimately, tremendous potential goes untapped.

Loss of Ego: The Power Ambition

Secretary of State Al Haig declared, "I'm in control here," to a stunned American audience just hours after the attempted assassination of President Reagan. The majority of Americans who watched the events unfold on that gloomy day were convinced by Haig's demeanor that his infamous line was deeply seeded in his personal desires to attain greater power. He was, after all, not truly in control of the presidency in such a crisis—that responsibility fell on the shoulders of Vice President George Bush. In the end, the comment would become a huge political liability Haig would never be able to overcome.

Whether Haig's comment was made solely in the effort to help calm the nation by assuring Americans that the government had someone in charge, or whether it was merely the unintended expression of his deeper ambitions for greater power and control in this moment of crisis, is a debate best left to his biographers. But if we accept the latter explanation, Al Haig is certainly by no means unique. Many who ascend to positions of great authority enjoy the power it brings while envying and desiring the greater powers they see in others. For many, whether in government or business, the power of being "in control" is personally very satisfying.

People rarely talk about their desire to gain power and control—it is a taboo subject, typically equated with blind, ego-centered ambition. It remains true, however, that this ego need is a strong motivator for many. HPWSs clearly suggest that power and control must be shared, not concentrated. For some, this equates to a loss of authority and stature that is very difficult to accept on a very personal level. For them, accepting HPWSs means subordinating their very ego.

FEAR OF EXPANSION

While some managers resist the transition to HPWSs because of the contraction spiral, seeing a greatly lessened role for themselves in the future, others resist for the opposite reason: They see the future as requiring the development of a new and diverse set of skills—skills they do not currently possess and may wonder whether they're capable of developing. This is a frightening proposition. Questions linger in their minds:

- Will I be able to learn what it takes to be successful?
- How much support will I get through this?

- HPWSs are completely outside my realm of experience—will I be able to adapt and manage in a different way?
- Do I have the savvy, desire, and energy to "go back to school" and start learning all over again?
- Even if I learn about HPWSs, what about my natural instincts? Won't I revert back to my old patterns as soon as things get tough or stressful?

The transition to HPWSs requires managers to step outside of their comfort zone and experiment with new roles and new working relationships. Like nearly any change that disrupts a long-standing and comfortable routine, there is considerable fear and anxiety associated with the transition. Much of the anxiety is a reflection of a lack of self-confidence. Many find the change overwhelming simply because they aren't sure they'll be able to adopt the new behaviors and techniques.

Too Much Change: Role Paralysis

"I don't understand it," confided a first-level manager. "I have these team meetings, but no one participates. The group just sits there like a bump on a log while I make all the decisions." After an independent observer attended one of his meetings, the problem became readily apparent. There was no meeting structure (no clearly defined purpose or agenda), his facilitation was ineffective (he dominated all discussions, rarely invited group members to participate, and was quick to judge the worth of their suggestions), and, in the rare instances where participation did occur, it was not given any positive reinforcement. After receiving feedback highlighting these factors and being presented with a specific plan for developing the necessary skills to become a more effective facilitator, the manager insisted that the team meetings had really improved since the initial observations. He also insisted that, while the suggestions were good, there wasn't any need to pursue the matter any further.

While this manager's behavior can be interpreted along several different lines, it seems most likely that at its core he had a lack of self-confidence in his ability as a team leader. In all probability the manager was initially hoping that the observer would confirm his perspective on the meetings: There was something wrong with the group. When the observer suggested that the problem was not with the group, but with the way the manager was playing out the role of facilitator, the need for change was suddenly transferred to his shoulders. It was he—not the group—that needed "fixing." His choice at this point was simple: Either accept the feedback and take the actions that had been recommended or ignore it. His decision to ignore it was probably rooted in a fear that he might not be able to develop the necessary facilitation skills, or that by going to a facilitation training session, his ineffectiveness at performing this aspect of the team leader role would become known to a broader audience within the company—possibly even his boss.

The fear of expansion often manifests itself in a kind of role paralysis. Managers resist experimenting with new behaviors, roles, and relationships out of the deep-seated anxiety that their inadequacies will be exposed. To them, the role expansion associated with HPWSs is not an opportunity for greater contribution but, rather, an opportunity for unwelcome visibility that could reveal their personal limitations.

ENDING THE DILEMMA IN THE MIDDLE

Overcoming the resistance associated with the fears of managers requires a concentrated effort early in the transition. In fact, the ideal approach is to practice *resistance prevention*. This is accomplished by anticipating the likely fears of managers and clearly addressing them before they become strengthened and ultimately detrimental to the transition. There are five tactics that are helpful in minimizing management resistance:

1. No Transition Layoffs

On February 13, 1989, more than five thousand managers from McDonnell Douglas's Commercial Airplane Division were invited to a meeting at one of the company's huge aircraft hangars. The attending managers had no idea what was going to be covered at the session. Many who stood in the enormous structure began speculating about why they had all been called together. In the minutes before the meeting, the room was rampant with rumors, but nothing being discussed or even imagined prepared the audience for what would actually follow. In the course of an hour the direction of the company and the loyalty of thousands would be changed forever.

Key executives explained that a new organization structure was needed to support the total-quality effort and assure increased work-force participation. Then an organization chart was presented that showed a greatly streamlined structure. Under the new structure, there would be a thousand fewer management positions. Further, to fill the four thousand positions that would remain, there would be a selection process requiring managers to apply for the available jobs. For those who weren't selected, the implication was clear—they would be laid off.

The audience was stunned. In the ensuing weeks utter chaos followed. Many no longer knew whom they reported to or even what their role was. One manager described how he had no fewer than five different managers during the course of the year following the infamous "Black Monday" announcement.

The transition at Mac Dac is a good example of what to avoid. In their attempt to help improve the company's performance, senior management made a direct connection between total quality/employee involvement and layoffs—a connection that greatly hurt the development of their TQM system. The enormous disruption and uncertainty caused by the announcement shook the loyalty of many employees who began aggressively seeking employment elsewhere (many would end up at McDonnell Douglas's archrival, Boeing). In the final analysis, the entire approach only served to heighten management resistance and hurt the speed and effectiveness of their transition.

A. O. Smith took a similar tack when it eliminated scores of first-line foremen. The ratio of foremen to workers went from 1:10 in 1987 to 1:34 during the 1989 team implementation. While the move did help reduce short-term overhead costs, the morale among the supervisors hit rock bottom and team performance began to slip.[8]

The champion of the change effort and appropriate senior managers need to make it clear that people will not be laid off as a result of the transition to HPWSs. The increased capacity gained by the productivity improvements will result in opportunities for managers to address strategic and competitive issues, not an opportunity to stand in the dole queue. The anticipated flattening of the organization will occur through effectively managing natural attrition. And while most managers will fill roles very different from the ones they performed prior to the transition, they will still have a job.

The promise of no layoffs as a result of making the transition to HPWSs should be distinguished from a "no-layoff guarantee." While no one will be laid off as a result of the transition, there remains the possibility that business viability could suffer for reasons unrelated to HPWSs (e.g., a sudden downturn in the economy). Under such severe circumstances, downsizing (including the possibility of layoffs) might be an option management would have to consider and possibly employ. Even IBM, with its full-employment tradition that dates back more than four decades, may ultimately end up in a position where layoffs are the only means left to preserve its viability, especially in light of its disastrous 1992 business performance. Most managers will readily recognize and appreciate this distinction.

Front-end assurances go a long way in lessening management

resistance. Managers at Steelcase, for instance, observed that the biggest mistake they made during their transition to HPWSs was in not letting supervisors know their employment would not be threatened by the change.[9] By letting managers know there will be work for them in the new system, progress toward gaining their commitment can begin.

2. Direct Involvement in the Transition Planning

A fundamental proposition of HPWSs can be stated as follows: Increased involvement leads to increased commitment. If we apply this to mid-managers, it translates into a simple strategy for gaining their commitment to HPWSs (and thereby lessening their resistance): Get them involved.

Early in the change effort a team needs to be put together that will coordinate the transition. The composition of the team should include the "key opinion leaders" from the middle-management ranks. This assures their direct involvement in the execution of the transition.

Direct involvement by mid-management on the transition team will help lessen their overall resistance. By having a meaningful role in defining the transition process, mid-managers begin developing a stronger vested interest in the success of the effort than in its failure.

3. Clear Definitions of the New Role

The words typically used to describe the role HPWS leaders play are woefully inadequate. One hears descriptors like *facilitator* and *resource*. The images these words conjure up in the minds of many managers evoke a sense of powerlessness and of giving in to the demands of others. The descriptors serve to perpetuate the belief that there is much to be lost and little to be gained by making the transition to HPWSs.

The transition must be viewed as an opportunity for role expansion. Organizations whose executives use the transition to

HPWSs as a means to cut costs by eliminating "white-collar fat" may be cutting out the very knowledge and capacity they will need for long-term survival. Rather than stress cutting, the emphasis should be on examining what the business will need to grow and prosper. Assuredly, the way to sustain growth is not by having everyone doing more of the same only at a faster rate. Growth requires new capabilities.

Simply telling mid-managers they can expect to see their role expand will not lessen their resistance. In the eyes of most, what they already have is of greater value than an ambiguous promise of what they might someday gain. The adage "One in the hand is worth two in the bush" exemplifies this commonsense pragmatism. So if we want mid-managers to willingly let go of what they have, they must first have something on which to take hold. Their new role needs to be clearly defined.

What kinds of roles have other companies seen their managers take on as teams began absorbing many of the traditional management responsibilities? Some left management entirely—typically to get back into a technical assignment. Others headed up special project teams like competitor tracking, market analysis, or strategic planning. Many became more directly—and formally—linked with customers and vendors, often serving on joint (customer/vendor) project teams. Others served as key members of a new-product development team. Many were rotated into other functions as a way to develop stronger general management capabilities within the company. And, of course, many became team leaders.

The role of team leader is particularly important to understand, for it requires a variety of competencies that have not necessarily been associated with managers and supervisors. In total, the team leader role has seven core attributes:

- *Leader*. Unleashing energy and enthusiasm by creating a motivating vision of a possible future and communicating group values and goals with tenacious consistency.

FIGURE 12: The Leader Model

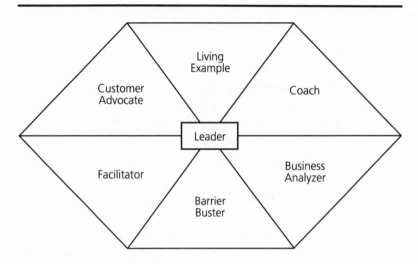

- *Living example.* Being a role model of effective interpersonal communication, teamwork, and consistency between espoused values and daily actions.
- *Coach.* Helping others develop to their fullest potential through training and personal support.
- *Business analyzer.* Understanding the environment surrounding the organization and developing strategy to take advantage of business opportunities.
- *Barrier buster.* Breaking down barriers that artificially limit the ability of the team to innovate and improve its performance.
- *Facilitator.* Providing the necessary resources, tools, and information to the team.
- *Customer advocate.* Working with customers to develop a full understanding of their desires and expectations of the products and/or services the team provides.

The team leader role requires a different set of abilities from those of the traditional manager. The classic role of planning, controlling, and directing must be replaced by leading, empowering, and coaching. Not all managers will be able to make this transition.

There will be some management turnover during the transition to HPWSs. Some will choose to leave on their own as part of the de-selection phenomenon, while a small percentage of others will be considered performance problems and be formally asked to depart. The number of managers who eventually leave will be determined by such factors as what other local job opportunities exist and the aggressiveness with which performance problems are addressed. For this reason the number of departing managers can vary dramatically—from about 5 percent of all managers on the low end to a full 25 percent on the high side. Despite these factors, it remains important that mid-managers clearly understand the nature of the new role expectations. Only then can they make an informed decision about whether it is in their best interest to support the transition or to seek out other opportunities.

4. Ongoing Information and Communication

For many managers the transition will be filled with concerns ranging from the superficial (what's going to happen to my reserved parking place?) to the substantive (what will be my real worth to this organization in the future?). During the transition many things will change—reporting structures, roles, systems, information channels, work design, and reward methods. During the initial phases of each of the changes, there will be an opportunity for misinformation and potentially destructive rumors.

Mid-managers are particularly susceptible to both receiving and giving tainted information. The reason? Senior management, in their effort to demonstrate their support for HPWSs, often bypass the middle in order to get more direct information sharing with those lower in the hierarchy. While this is an important demonstration of senior-management convictions, many mid-level managers instantly interpret this as demonstrating their lack of importance to the new order. Just like the childhood game of telephone, as original information gets told and retold, it continually gets distorted. The mid-manager who is hearing second- or third-hand about a presentation a vice president made to a production group may have a completely wrong interpretation of what was actually said. If one of the issues discussed was relevant to mid-managers, there will be a tendency to put a more negative interpretation on the words than what was intended. This, in turn, gets interpreted and retold. Misinformation begets *enhanced misinformation* until—in the extreme—wild rumors begin circulating that have no foundation in fact.

The most obvious way to combat this vicious cycle is to consciously maintain open communication channels with all levels in the organization. While it will be important at times to target communications at certain groups, there should never be the feeling that something is being held back or purposely not shared with middle management. The tendency to not include mid-management has occurred in so many transitions that it can be characterized as an often harmful but natural tendency. Often the importance of their role in supporting the change is not immediately recognized. They are not directly involved in "championing the change," as are the senior-level managers; they do not see the same kind of immediate role shift that is expected among supervisors and first-level managers; and they do not see the expansion in authority and responsibility that the rest of the work force experiences. As attention is focused on other aspects of the implementation and mid-management is largely ignored, their skepticism, misunderstanding, and resistance increase. Concentration on conveying information to the middle ranks will lessen resistance by keeping misinformation and destructive rumors at bay.

5. *Training and Support*

HPWSs require fundamental changes in the entire practice of management. Given this fact, it would be unrealistic to assume that hordes of middle managers are suddenly going to "get it" and immediately start behaving in ways that are substantially different from what they learned in their business school or management experience. There are numerous skills and abilities managers must learn, practice, and apply.

There must be a commitment to provide education and training to managers—and, in most cases, this means a sizable investment. Remarkably, most major corporations spend a tiny fraction of their budget on training. In hard times, training is typically one of the first line items to get cut. HPWSs will require a reversal of this mentality. Human assets must be thought of as a distinct competitive advantage. Failing to provide ongoing education to managers must be thought of as being as ridiculous as buying a new computer and never plugging it in. For the organization to ascend toward its potential, it must have managers well trained in the skills required in a HPWS. The painful fact for many cost-conscious executives is that this could likely mean doubling or even tripling the amount of money and time that goes into education and training.

The new skills that managers must develop all relate to operating in a team-based, rather than an individual-based, environment. While this list is by no means comprehensive, it is indicative of what those in the middle will need to know to flourish in a HPWS.

- Effective meeting management skills
- How to develop and manage by using boundary conditions
- How to develop and utilize operating guidelines
- How to facilitate groups
- Skills for coaching a team
- Skills for coaching individuals
- How to set goals and measurements as a team
- Reaching effective decisions in a team
- How to utilize process observations to improve team effectiveness
- How to develop and present education and training

- How to deal with interface issues between teams
- Resolving team conflicts
- Resolving individual conflict
- Problem-solving processes
- Problem-solving tools
- Work redesign techniques
- How to challenge and remove organization barriers
- How to develop and sustain close customer ties
- How to develop and sustain close vendor ties
- Effective action planning
- Recognizing business trends and their likely impact
- Upgrading of technical knowledge and skills

THE LEAP OF FAITH

Dealing with the "middle-management issue" must be a central concern in planning out the organization-wide transition to HPWSs. More than any other single group, mid-management can play the pivotal role in assuring that the transition is successful, or they can serve to create enormous barriers that will ultimately kill it. And yet despite the tremendous impact they can and will ultimately have on the transition, there is a seemingly natural tendency to ignore their ranks during the planning process. It is as if there is an underlying assumption that mid-managers will be good soldiers and follow the direction of senior management. This assumption may be true to an extent, but at the point where mid-managers see their role threatened—either by substantial contraction in responsibilities or excessive expansion in expectations—there will be a tendency for them to deviate from their orders and focus on what they see as the requirements for self-preservation.

The best way to eliminate mid-management resistance to HPWSs is to stop it before it begins—in effect, to practice prevention. By focusing early in the effort on eliminating several of the sources of resistance—such as the fears of losing employment, of having a diminished role, or of having new, greatly expanded responsibilities—mid-management support will be more easily gained. Gaining this support is not without its short-term costs: There will be no immediate salary reductions from layoffs, and it is likely the education and training budget could increase two- or threefold. The gamble—what for some might better be characterized as a leap of faith—is that the longer-term gains of increasing mid-management support, and thereby increasing the speed and likely success of the transition to HPWSs, will offset these initial costs. While there are literally hundreds of other factors that will ultimately determine the success of the transition, by not taking the leap, the organization is almost assuredly guaranteed mediocre results.

CHAPTER 8

Creating the Working Blueprint

Infuriated, the head of engineering challenged the division vice president: "There is no way self-directed work teams or whatever you want to call them can work in my department, so stop harping on it. You simply can't cross-train every engineer the way you can cross-train assembly operators—it just can't be done!"

The engineering manager had a good point: How can a software engineer be expected to develop hardware engineering skills? With the rapidity of new knowledge entering their respective fields, by the time the software engineer is fully trained in intricacies of developing hardware (about a five-year education commitment), his or her software skills would be teetering on the edge of obsolescence. Besides the fact that it would be impractical and costly to execute such cross-training, it would require superhuman efforts by all those involved to stay abreast of the latest developments in their first discipline while attempting to learn a second (or third or fourth) area of expertise.

Unfortunately, there is a widespread belief that in a high performance team every team member can do every other member's job with the same degree of skill and knowledge. Underlying this perspective is the assumption that the benefit from creating a team occurs only when team members are completely inter-changeable. While this is desirable in some settings, it is not practical (or even desirable) in others. It is but one model of how teams can work effectively.

A major problem in many work redesign efforts is that the wrong *team model* is being used. The implementers of these mis-guided efforts are doing the equivalent of pounding a square peg into a round hole—they are force-fitting one type of team into a situation where it simply is not appropriate. The predictable result is often a costly failure, characterized by poor team perfor-mance and high levels of frustration among team members.

In all there are four basic types of work teams, each with certain strengths and certain weaknesses that can prove helpful or detri-mental to the HPWS transition. A critical first step in forming a high performance work team is to be very clear about which model of teaming is the best fit given the requirements of the work to be performed.

THE CHOIR

In the 1970s Volvo introduced a completely new concept in automobile manufacturing in their plant in Kalmar, Sweden. Rather than have individuals do the same repetitive task over and over again at a single station along the assembly line (like bolting down a bumper or tightening lug nuts), Volvo created work teams that were responsible for building entire cars. For auto-mobile manufacturing the approach was revolutionary—so much so that in the late Seventies executives from Volvo were asked to testify before the U.S. Congress about why they had adopted the "team" approach and the benefits they had gained from it.

The teams at Volvo became a symbol of a new concept of work design that assured total employee involvement. It was a unique approach in two respects. First, it focused on a whole piece of

FIGURE 13: Team Typology

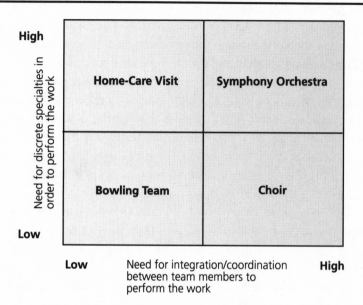

work rather than on discrete tasks, and second, it utilized teams with highly cross-trained members who were able to fill in for any other member at any point in the production process. A new and exciting model of work had been created that was soon being applied to a variety of industries across North America and Europe. For many it would become the definitive example of how a high performance team operates.

A team focused on completing a "whole" piece of work, with team members all sharing comparable skills, functions much the same way a choir does. For a choir to perform, all members must have—at a minimum—the common skill of singing and the common knowledge of the words to be sung. In this sense the choir is cross-trained, every member is fully capable of singing the same words as any other member. If one member of the choir is absent, the impact on the choir as a whole is minimal—in effect, others fill in for the missing person. While each choir member has a common base set of skills and knowledge, his or her ability to sing in unity requires a high level of coordination. The same words must be sung at the same time, in the same key, and at the same rhythm.

The two factors that make a choir unique from other types of teams are: (1) a high level of common knowledge and skills among its members, and (2) a high level of member coordination. Other analogous teams with similar characteristics would include a volleyball team or a doubles tennis team—in these examples every member of the team can perform all the necessary functions while a high level of coordination is necessary for the successful execution of the work. In business, *choirs* work best when a team can be responsible for a whole piece of work (such as building an entire product or combining various tasks into a single work cell) and cross-training can occur over a relatively short time horizon (usually within one to two years).

The choir approach has been most widely used in manufacturing settings. At several Hewlett-Packard plants, for example, employees are multiskilled to the point where they can build and test an entire instrument. Procter & Gamble's plant in Lima, Ohio, encourages employees to become cross-trained in every skill area required to keep the plant running. The effectiveness of the choir approach begins to break down when the need for coordination among team members is minimal or in instances where it would be nearly impossible or impractical for each team member to be cross-trained in the skills of other team members. In these instances other approaches to teaming are far more effective.

THE SYMPHONY ORCHESTRA

A symphony is made up of a number of different and unique skill sets. There are the wind section, the string section, and the percussionists. To become proficient at any one of these instrument families requires years of dedicated practice and study. An orchestra, unlike a choir, is made up of individuals with discrete and varied skills.

For an orchestra to successfully perform a concert, its body of specialists must coordinate their efforts. Failure by any instrument section to play at the right time or in the right key will disrupt the entire performance. It is the coordination of the various specialized skills that creates the magical sound of Beethoven or Mozart.

A symphony orchestra is different from other types of teams in that it requires (1) a high level of unique and varied knowledge and skills among its members, and (2) a high level of coordination. In general, businesses and governmental organizations have been good at developing top-caliber specialists. This is particularly true in the United States, which boasts the most expert-intensive work force—with more Ph.D.'s and master's degrees—of any country in the world. Yet while the U.S. may have the best and brightest in a number of fields, its competitive slippage in many key industries (from consumer electronics to steel to automobiles) is widely recognized. Why? Because most companies don't behave like an orchestra—there is no integration of ideas and skills toward a unified whole. Having the greatest intellectual power in the marketing department, the engineering department, and the manufacturing department will not ensure a competitive advantage in the marketplace if there is no coordination and integration of effort.

In recent years there has been a tremendous amount of interest in cross-functional teams as a way to assure that specialties are integrated and working toward a common goal. At Tektronix, cross-functional teams were used extensively in new-product development efforts. The results were astounding—a two-year reduction in time-to-market. These teams had representatives from engineering (hardware and software), manufacturing (including assembly and procurement), finance, marketing, and human resources. Fisher Controls is undergoing an effort to enhance its entire systems-release process by forming cross-functional core teams that are completely responsible for coordinating all the elements of the company's systems-release process. These teams contract with other functional groups—like engineering or manufacturing—to support specific aspects of the release. In a sense they are the conductor, carefully integrating all the knowledge and skill of the various functional groups into a new system offering for Fisher's customers. Chrysler's LH car was designed by a team that included representation from every major department—engineering, styling, marketing, manufacturing—as well as several key suppliers. The resulting "cab forward" design—which required a complete rethinking of engine placement, windshield design, and wheelbase distance—has been touted by many as the most significant advancement in automotive design in over a decade.

An orchestra requires strong and effective leadership. The leader helps coordinate the activities of the various specialists and keeps them focused on the grander goal. Orchestra teams work best when the nature of work requires expertise and skills from several different disciplines and there is a high need for the efforts of the specialists to be coordinated for a successful outcome. In business settings, orchestra teams have been used most extensively in new-product and/or new-service development efforts. More recently, the model has been applied during redesign efforts where the new organization structure is based on core processes (requiring the formation of teams with members from a variety of specialized disciplines) rather than on discrete functions (like engineering, marketing, finance or human resources).

THE HOME-CARE VISIT

Consider the team approach used by many home-care agencies. Several different members of the home-care team will visit a patient at various times over the course of several days or weeks.

The patient might, for example, see a registered nurse on Monday, a physical therapist on Tuesday, a dietitian on Wednesday, a social worker on Thursday, and a housecleaner on Friday. In this team model each member is providing his or her unique expertise and skill to help the patient improve or, in the case of the terminally ill, to help the patient die in comfort and with a sense of dignity. While the nature of the work that the team is performing requires a high level of specialization, the need to integrate their various efforts is somewhat secondary. While actually visiting the patient, the provider is focused on fulfilling the prescribed treatment plan for his or her unique area of expertise regardless of what the specialist who came before or the one coming after will be providing.

There is clearly a need for coordination among the various home-care specialists. The social worker, for example, needs to be aware of the side effects medications might have on the person's mental state—information that can be given in detail by the RN. This is usually accomplished by the rigid maintenance of the patient chart and weekly team meetings, but compared to the symphony orchestra model, the home-care team needs far less integration and coordinated effort in order to successfully perform its work. They are a team with highly differentiated skills and areas of expertise and a relatively low need for immediate integration of their activities.

In a business setting, the home-care model is commonly used—sometimes in settings where it is inappropriate. Its potential weakness is that it deemphasizes coordination when, in fact, coordination might greatly enhance overall performance. Take a phone bank that receives orders for a catalog business as an example. Following the home-care model, there might be several specialists—one who enters orders, another who specializes in providing information about products, a third who handles questions relating to exchanges and refunds, and a fourth who takes care of complaints. Customers calling in may find it annoying to be transferred several times based on the type of question they have—they want the inquiry addressed immediately, preferably by a single individual. In this setting a choir team, where any member of the phone team can address the majority of customer inquiries, is probably a better and more effective model.

THE BOWLING TEAM

The last teaming example operates like a bowling team. The members of a bowling team have a set of common skills (they can all bowl), but the team's performance requires very little coordination among its membership (they each bowl independently of other team members). In effect, each bowler is performing an action or job (bowling) that requires no participation from any other team member for its successful completion.

Bank tellers are an example of the bowling model in a work setting. Each teller performs the same job and has essentially the same skills. The teller executes his or her function with very little need for coordination with any other team member—in fact, the teller operates in relative isolation from others.

When is the bowling model the appropriate approach? In instances where work requires common skills among several team members but there is little need for them to regularly coordinate their efforts. As with the home-care model, however, the advantages of integrating and/or coordinating activities should be carefully assessed before picking this model of teaming. Wouldn't tellers benefit, for example, from having regular meetings during which they could share strategies for addressing customer complaints or discuss ways to speed up transactions so that customers spend less time in line and more time being served? Regular meetings would be one example of an integrating mechanism that could help improve individual and team performance.

There is no right or wrong type of team—each teaming model has various strengths and weaknesses depending on the nature of the work the team will be performing. In some settings the bowling model will be the most appropriate, while in others it will be the symphony, choir, or home-care model. The key is to match the nature of the work to the form of team that will best perform it. Don't put in a home-care team because it's easier and cheaper to implement when a choir is what's really needed to improve performance over the long run.

WHEN IS A TEAM A TEAM?

The four fundamentally different types of teams we just looked at are based on two defining characteristics: the need for coordination of actions among team members and the degree of specialized or discrete skills needed within the team to perform. Regardless of the type of team (i.e., choir, orchestra, home-care, or bowling), there are common characteristics all team configurations have that clearly differentiate them from groups or collections of individuals. This is an important distinction: Many companies are using the bowling or home-care model to form groups, but in no way have they created a fully functioning team.

A team has a common:

- Purpose
- Understanding of how the activities of the team link to the company
- Awareness of the customer needs that the team's efforts are addressing
- Understanding of team member roles
- Information-sharing, problem-solving, and decision-making mechanisms
- Set of operating guidelines or norms of behavior

Regardless of the type of team, these factors remain common—they are the defining qualities of teaming. Without them, there is no team, merely a collection of individuals.

IMPLEMENTATION STRATEGY

Defining the type of team model(s) must be closely followed by developing an overall implementation strategy for how to put the teams in place. The appropriate strategy must be a reflection of both the forces necessitating the change and the opportunities that exist within the organization. Martin Marietta's Astronautics Group, for example, used a "blitz" strategy—a massive organization-wide effort that left virtually nothing untouched. During the course of a mere nine months, more than eight thousand employees were trained in the principles of high performance and teams were implemented across the entire organization. The speed and sheer size of the effort sent managers reeling for cover. In sharp contrast, Fisher Controls began its effort by forming three six-member core teams. The members of these teams represented a cross-functional slice of the organization (engineering, marketing, sales, manufacturing). These teams—given the responsibility to manage all aspects of Fisher's systems-release process—were islands surrounded by a sea of traditional functional organizations. The strategy was to use the learning from the core team experience to help spread high performance work systems across the rest of Fisher. In effect, the "islands" would help in the transformation of the "nation."

There are a four common strategies that can be employed when introducing HPWSs. Each approach has unique advantages and disadvantages. They are:

1. Greenfield (a new plant start-up)
2. Island to nation (begin with a small group and then slowly

expand the implementation effort across the rest of the organization)

3. Piggyback (introduce the change simultaneously with some other major process or organizational change)

4. Blitz (a top-down implementation effort in which the focus of the effort is the total organization)

GREENFIELD

For years the literature relating to HPWSs was dominated by examples from new plant start-ups. These became known as "greenfield" plants—the term originating from the fact that the new plants were often built on former farmland where great fields of corn, alfalfa, or other "green" crops once stood. Many of these efforts have been highly effective and much publicized. The Procter & Gamble plant in Lima, Ohio, the Gaines Food plant in Topeka, Kansas, the former Digital Equipment plant in Enfield, Connecticut, and the Tektronix circuit board facility in Forest Grove, Oregon, are four well-known examples of successful greenfield efforts.

A new plant start-up offers many advantages in implementing HPWS methods. First, there is no preexisting work culture or tradition. There is a clear advantage in working with a clean slate than with existing plants, which have organizational norms and accepted behaviors that are often inconsistent with increased employee involvement. In some organizations, the work culture has become such a destructive, antiparticipative force that it leads to the venting of frustrations in many bizarre and destructive ways: wall graffiti, tire slashing, and even the need for bulletproof glass! By contrast, in the new plant the work culture is not a victim of its past. It can be carefully, consciously designed from the beginning. The same is true of support systems. The way information is disseminated, the way work is designed, and the way rewards are given out can all be developed consistent with the HPWS principles from the very beginning of the operation. Second, there is far less resistance to change during a start-up since people do not perceive themselves as losing any status or authority, as is often the case during the redesign of an existing operation. Status barriers can be eliminated by simply not allowing perquisites and other symbols or forms of favoritism in the new design. Eliminating these same perks in a preexisting organization is often seen as a reduction of well-deserved entitlements.

Despite the many advantages, greenfields are fairly rare events because of the cost associated with starting up a new facility. Companies that are interested in experimenting with HPWSs simply do not go out and start up a new plant. In those instances where a company is planning to build a new facility, it is a natural place to introduce HPWSs. (It's noteworthy that greenfield plants have been reported to outproduce traditionally designed facilities by a 20 to 40 percent margin.) Most organizations, however, do not have the luxury of starting up a new facility. For them the question becomes, how do we implement HPWSs into our current operations?

ISLAND TO NATION

The next three strategies are related to introducing HPWSs in an existing organization. The first is the "island to nation" strategy. In this strategy, a single prototype or experimental group (the island) is developed into a highly effective team. The lessons learned from this "island" experiment are then applied during the formation and transition of other groups to HPW teams. Eventually, because of the number of HPW teams operating within the organization, a kind of critical mass is reached and substantive changes to the organization as a whole (the nation) occur at an accelerated pace. In effect, what starts as the adoption of HPWSs at the single group level eventually spreads across the entire department, plant, division, or even company!

The island-to-nation strategy is low risk since an early failure means that only a relatively small part of the organization—the single prototype or "island" group, which typically is no more than six to twenty members—will be directly affected. For this reason it is a particularly appealing strategy to managers who are both curious and skeptical about HPWSs. The approach allows them to take a look at HPWSs before making a major organizational, financial, and personal commitment to it. Unfortunately, this appealing characteristic is also this strategy's nemesis. When an island team encounters difficulty or runs into organizational barriers that hurt its effectiveness, the temptation for some managers is to quickly cut off the effort rather than deal with the broader gut-wrenching issues such as span of control, roles, department charters, status, and restructuring. With the consequences for stopping the effort relatively painless, the first sign of trouble sends many of the skeptics down the path of least resistance—it is far easier to maintain the status quo than to reform it.

There are two other related problems with the island-to-nation approach. First, there is no such thing as a true "island" in an organization—every group has some level of interdependency with other groups. As an example, let's say we decide to implement this strategy, for illustrative purposes, on the Pegasus manufacturing line. After several months of learning about HPWSs and holding regular team problem-solving meetings, the group develops a redesign plan for the work area to improve efficiency. The industrial engineering group hears of this move and insists that all work redesign must come from their office. The quality organization says it cannot be done without their approval because a change in the work flow will disrupt the statistical process charts they have developed to monitor quality. The employees on the two neighboring manufacturing lines want to know why the

Pegasus employees are "special" and "have meetings all the time" instead of "working to get product out like they're supposed to." The point is that you really cannot change one group in isolation because of the great number of interdependencies that exist between it and other groups. The reality is that the interdependencies must also be considered and managed if the effort is to succeed.

The second problem with this strategy centers around a widely held assumption that is false. The assumption goes like this: If an experimental group is successful at becoming a HPWS, others will quickly replicate it and create HPW teams of their own. In actual fact, the opposite reaction is far more common: The initial response by managers to successful "islands" is to suggest that the island team is somehow unique ("the type of work they perform lends itself better to a team set-up") or has had certain advantages that do not commonly exist among other groups in the organization ("the people on that team were handpicked"). Actually this response is natural if we understand it from the perspective of a group manager. By replicating what a peer has done as a model for improved performance is to imply that one's peer is a better manager than oneself—an admission that could be career-damaging. The natural recourse is to suggest that the island manager has had certain advantages or unusual circumstances that enabled her to be successful. This tendency is so common it even has a name: "the not-invented-here syndrome."

There is no question that the success of an island has the potential to help lessen resistance to HPWSs, but success alone will not create a sudden and dramatic flurry to the HPWS camp—a fact that many implementers have found both puzzling and discouraging. As we have seen, though, this reaction is both predictable and likely. This same phenomenon operates on a more macro-level. Procter & Gamble, for example, has had over two decades of side-by-side comparisons showing that their plants with "enlightened work systems" outperform their traditional plants in virtually every key measure (e.g., quality, customer service, reliability), including a consistent showing of 30 to 50 percent lower manufacturing costs. Despite the overwhelming proof of superior performance, the traditional plants have been slow to replicate the techniques, structures, and processes of the high performing ones.

Can the island-to-nation strategy work? The answer is clearly "yes." Within IBM Canada Ltd. much of the early work on HPWSs started in two small periphery organizations—a fifty-person sales branch in Vancouver, British Columbia, and a one-hundred-person software lab in Toronto, Ontario. These two efforts became models for other efforts within the IBM system across Canada. The idea has spread to customer service locations, education and training, the quality institute, finance, manufacturing operations, and several additional sales branches and software labs. Corning, Shell, and a host of others have also used the strategy with considerable success in spreading HPWSs to other groups within the company.

For the manager who wants to experiment with HPWSs, forming a relatively small island team (six to twenty members) can serve as an impressive proving ground. By creating a highly focused team, impressive results—with the right leadership and a well thought-through implementation plan—can be achieved in a relatively short time frame. But the success of the island does not mean HPWSs will be adopted across a wider audience within the company. For the formation of an island to lead to a substantial change across the organization, several factors must be present:

1. Unyielding Focus on the Ends

A "wait and see" approach will not be enough to sustain the change. The champion and the members of the team helping to plan out the implementation must make it clear from the beginning how island teams will be formed and used as vehicles to reshape the entire organization. The ends—a high performing, team-based organization—are what must be emphasized. The formation of each new island team is a milestone along the way to creating a new work culture at the department, plant, division, or company level.

2. Nurture and Support

Invariably, there will be barriers, some of which will be debilitating for the early teams. Many can be predicted (e.g., cost-accounting systems that penalize managers for the time team members are in meetings, training, and other "nonproduction" activities). Other barriers will drop, unanticipated, out of the blue (e.g., an angry vendor wanting to know why an operator called him with a complaint rather than the group manager). It is important that the team receives lots of support in overcoming these barriers—whatever form they might take.

3. A Formal Process for Shared Learning

The efficiency and effectiveness of team implementation need to continually improve. This can be achieved by structuring information-sharing forums during which the early, "pioneer" teams can share their experiences with the later, "settler" teams. The pioneers need to be held accountable for not only the success of HPWSs within their team, but across the entire organization as well.

4. Utilization of the "Black Hole Phenomenon"

The best place to form the first island is at the core of the value-adding chain. In a manufacturing company, this would be with a group building a product on the manufacturing line. In a service organization, it would be with a group that is providing services directly to customers. The reason for starting here is simple: Changes to the core processes will quickly get the attention of and require a response from support organizations. Joe Burger, a former general manager at Tektronix, calls this the "black hole phenomenon"—by focusing early changes on the core work areas, an extreme gravitational pull is created requiring a reaction from support groups. In contrast, first adopting a high performance team within a support organization, say the human-resources department, will get little attention and create virtually no pull for change in other groups.

For the island-to-nation strategy to be successful in transforming a plant, division, or company into a HPWS, these four factors need to be carefully considered. Simply forming a small team and demonstrating how effective HPW techniques are at improving performance will, in most instances, do little—if anything—to lead the larger organization down the path of change.

PIGGYBACK

A fundamental principle in organization theory can be stated as follows: For organization change to occur, there must be an "unfreezing" of the status quo—a temporary state where the organization is malleable enough for new systems and processes to be introduced. This idea is important to consider because it helps explain why so many efforts at change are unsuccessful. Many change efforts are attempted when the organization is still "frozen"; the so-called change agents are merely moving boxes around without any fundamental change to the organization's values, systems, processes, or technologies.

In most organizations there are a multitude of "unfreezing" events that occur each year. Included would be the introduction of a major new technology or process; a sudden and dramatic increase or decline in sales; the introduction of a new product; the creation of a new function, department, or manufacturing line; or a shake-up of the executive office. Any of these changes might unfreeze the organization enough to help lessen the resistance to change. Tying the implementation of HPWSs to any one of these events can help speed its acceptance and likely longevity within the organization.

The dramatic improvements made at Microsoft's manufacturing facility in Dublin, Ireland, serve as a vivid example. Brian Reynolds, the GM of Ireland, recognized the numerous inefficiencies in their disk duplication and packaging process. To make matters worse, inventory turns were painstakingly slow due to the enormous amounts of inventory in their storage area. This added significantly to cost since any software upgrade had the potential to leave thousands of user manuals and other supporting documentation obsolete. The work design followed an assembly-line model, with workers confined to performing narrowly defined jobs in the duplication room, the storage area, or on the production line. In many ways, the entire manufacturing design was in the dark ages, using the best techniques of the sixties and seventies.

Reynolds set out to turn the operation into a world-class manufacturer. The emphasis was on improving business performance through the introduction of Just-in-Time manufacturing techniques. It was immediately recognized that instituting Just-in-Time was going to require significant changes in manufacturing processes, relationships with vendors, technologies—even changes in the commonly held philosophy of how to manufacture and package Microsoft products. The disruption this created in the organization served to unfreeze it and make it malleable to change. Many of the systems and processes, including the way management had traditionally operated, began to be questioned. This created an ideal opportunity for tying high performance work practices to the world-class manufacturing effort. The assembly line, for example, gave way to the formation of thirty work cells—or choir teams—that were completely responsible for all aspects of production. HPWSs, in essence, "piggybacked" on the unfreezing effect of the world-class manufacturing effort.

At Northern Telecom the unfreezing event is a worldwide emphasis on quality through a program called "Excellence!" In implementing this effort, the company has combined it with many of the facets of HPWSs in trying to create a sustainable quality culture. Boston Whaler, the renowned manufacturer of "unsinkable" commercial and pleasure boats, has, in recent years, aggressively pursued cost reduction. They quickly recognized the power of including the team concept as part of their strategy for gaining implementable solutions for lowering costs. In each of these cases, HPWSs were combined with some other major change initiative focused at improving bottom-line performance. The intent was not to implement HPWSs, but to improve manufacturing, quality, or cost. By piggybacking HPWSs on these other initiatives, however, the effectiveness of the effort was strengthened.

If there is a major effort to improve quality, lower costs, restructure the business, install Just-in-Time disciplines, or improve customer service, it is a natural fit to piggyback HPWSs on the effort. In fact, the effort may not succeed without the benefits of the piggybacking *effect*.

BLITZ

"Blitz" describes a total organization-wide change in which the effort encompasses the total system (whether it be a plant, division, or company) all at once. It is similar to a greenfield approach, where the total organization must be designed, with one significant difference: Since the organization is already functioning, with a long history and deeply rooted organization culture, the task is doubly difficult. Unlike with a new plant start-up, one cannot realistically spend large amounts of time with the work force and managers in planning and training sessions. They must be producing products and/or providing services rather than working out the details of a transition to HPWSs. Thus a catch-22 emerges: How do you change if you don't have the time to plan out the change or educate people about it?

Part of the answer is that managers and the members of the groups they manage must become very clever about more effectively utilizing the time that is available for training. But the other half of the answer is that time and budget must be created if the entire system is to be changed. Many organizations that have implemented HPWSs in this manner saw declines in performance during most of the implementation phase—the result of large amounts of training and meeting time that were not immediately offset by performance improvements. While such declines don't always occur, immediate short-term performance improvement when utilizing a blitz strategy is far more difficult to attain due to the size of the system that is being transformed. Managers who lack confidence in the approach—and who will undoubtedly feel additional pressure for short-term improvements from their superiors—may find themselves quickly returning to their old patterns of management and wounding the change. It takes a high level of commitment to weather out what can be very tough storms during the transition.

Since the total organization is being taken on at once, the stakes are notably higher and the pathway to success notably more difficult. This is clearly the implementation approach with the highest element of risk and the highest potential fast payoff since the total organization is being changed on an accelerated timeline.

One of the biggest organizations ever to attempt a blitz was Martin Marietta's Astronautics Group. In less than a year, everyone in the organization attended introductory training describing what a high performance work team was and how roles would need to dramatically change for it to be successful. Managers were given follow-up training, and an organization effectiveness group was formed for the sole purpose of supporting the effort across the nearly ten-thousand-person division. Teams were formalized, each creating a charter that related to its specific role in helping create space-launch vehicles. Team meetings soon became a regular part of the workday.

The results of the effort were both extraordinary and frustrating. Estimates in cost savings as a direct result of going to HPWTs were put at nearly $10 million. On the down side, a fraction of the hundreds of teams that were formed directly contributed to the cost savings. A kind of bipolar distribution had evolved—teams with extraordinary performance and countless improvement ideas and those where there was little discernible change or improvement over the way the group had operated prior to the change. The reason for this imbalance was related to the sheer size of the effort and the limited number of organization effectiveness resources to help those groups that were struggling. While senior management clearly viewed the effort as a success, the potential that was left untapped is truly daunting.

Martin Marietta's experience points out several requirements that are needed for a successful blitz implementation. These include:

- A significant budget allowance for training and meeting time
- Dedicated resources whose primary role is to help the newly formed teams operate effectively
- Tenacious support from the champion
- A willingness to accept short-term declines in performance
- A strong commitment to remove barriers that are hurting team performance

It is also important to consider the size of the organization that will be undergoing the transition. As size increases, the complexities associated with a blitz implementation go up exponentially! Ideally, implementation efforts involving more than five hundred or one thousand employees would be phased in over time. Attempting an effort where thousands would be affected all at once—without an extraordinary level of resources and support—will likely create some pockets of success and some of failure.

A colleague refers to the blitz strategy as "trying to change your tire while you're still riding the bicycle." In many ways his description is accurate. The blitz approach requires tremendous coordination, a heavy concentration of resources, and a high tolerance for risk.

PICKING A STRATEGY

Each strategy—from greenfield to blitz—has certain requirements and can provide specific advantages over the others depending on circumstances surrounding the organization undergoing the change. It is important in determining the most appropriate strategy to consider:

- Available resources. How much money and personnel can be applied toward this effort?
- Existing opportunities. Is there a new plant start-up imminent? Is there a major initiative about to be announced that could serve as a piggyback opportunity?
- Tolerance for risk. How much are individuals willing to risk? Their careers?
- Business conditions. How fast must the organization attain significant improvements in performance? Is the speed of the implementation an issue of survival for the company?

THE WORKING BLUEPRINT

The working blueprint for implementing HPWSs begins with two important elements:

1. A determination of what type(s) of team(s) is most appropriate to meet the demands the organization is facing
2. An overall strategy for how to get them in place and operating

As we have seen, there are lots of options to consider, each with varying strengths and weaknesses. Each has the potential for success or the potential for failure.

Many efforts fall apart because the would-be implementers have a simplistic perspective of how the teams should be structured. A common mistake is to think of all teams as needing to fit a single team model—that is neither realistic nor true. Within the same division, *choir* teams were used to manufacture products, the *symphony orchestra* model was used for new-product development efforts, and the *home-care* model was used as the primary form in the sales organization. The "best" team configuration was determined by the nature of the work each group was expected to perform. The adage "Form follows function" captures the point—define the purpose of the team first and then determine the most appropriate teaming model.

To a large extent the same is true of picking the right implementation strategy. Pursuing a high-risk blitz implementation, for example, can prove disastrous if substantial resources are not available to support the effort. The chosen strategy must be a reflection of the current conditions and perceived opportunities that reside within the organization.

The intent of the working blueprint is to develop a sense of how the organization will be structured and how the transition will unfold. While the blueprint gives us a framework, innumerable questions remain—questions that will have to be addressed as the transition unfolds:

- How will information be disseminated? Who will have access to what?
- How will work be designed? Who will be responsible for it?
- What kind of training will be required?
- How will rewards be allocated? What changes will need to be made to the compensation system?

Successfully developing the working blueprint marks an important milestone in the transition. Despite the many questions and obstacles that remain, the emerging HPWS now has a foundation of support.

CHAPTER 9

The Information
Transfer

As a young supervisor in the 1960s, Goodyear's Ed Finnan can remember being told by his manager to never interact with the employees who worked for him. "Your job," Finnan's manager would say matter-of-factly, "is to make sure they are busy and not cheating on us. That's it." The message was very clear: Information should be shared only on a need-to-know basis. Like it or not, keeping people "in the dark" was simply part of being a good manager.

Many things have changed at Goodyear through the years—Finnan now teaches managers how to empower their employees. His work represents the new Goodyear, a company that is aggressively trying to gain a performance advantage by utilizing HPWTs.

Many organizations have not progressed so far. In some companies employees cannot give an answer to the simple question "What is it your company does?" There is often little identification with the product or service since many employees are asked to focus all their attention on performing narrowly defined tasks. While becoming experts at performing the specific tasks they are assigned, they often have little understanding of the greater business picture. Basic questions are left unanswered:

- What is the finished product used for?
- What are the expectations of customers?
- Who are the competitors and what differentiates their product/ services from ours?
- What is the financial performance of the business?
- How does my work relate to the work of others in my work group?
- What is the quality of my work?
- With whom do I share my improvement ideas?
- Why can't I have a say in decisions?

As an operator at Kodak, recalling the days before the 13 Room teams were formed, noted, "You were literally told what to do and how to do it. You never got any information about the business or even how the unit was performing. You were completely in the dark. And if you didn't follow up on a demand you'd been given and the supervisor found out about it, the comment back would be 'You don't need a pass to leave here, only to get in.'"

To create highly cohesive, high performing teams, people within the organization must genuinely feel as if they are business partners and not mere cogs in the great corporate wheel. It would be unthinkable for any rational person to willingly enter a business partnership if he did not know anything about the product or services the company provided, had no idea what the customers expected, knew nothing about who the key competitors were or what the organization's financial performance was. Yet historically, these very same business basics are rarely shared with members of the work force. A self-fulfilling prophecy emerges: Employees don't seem to care about the company because they are treated as if there is nothing they should care about.

INFORMATION TECHNOLOGY—THE DARK SIDE

It is ironic that as the costs associated with information sharing have spiraled downward—thanks to the dramatic price reductions that have occurred over the last two decades in virtually every facet of information technology—barriers that profoundly limit who has access to business information within companies have remained remarkably strong. In the extreme, some have even used the tools of the information revolution to create controls and surveillance techniques that would humble Orwell. Instead of seeing easier and cheaper access to information as a means to enhance organization responsiveness and employee commitment, it has been used as a spying device.

At the site of a major chemical producer in the United Kingdom, a card key system was installed so that the location of any employee could be immediately determined in the event of a spill or fire. The system was heralded by management and labor alike as a significant tool for helping focus the efforts of rescuers in the event of a plant disaster. But while the card key system could help save lives, it also had the potential to provide management with information that was of a more sinister nature. The system could be used to monitor how long an employee was at a meeting, the amount of time he took for lunch, how long his breaks were, even the amount of time spent in the restroom! The temptation among the management staff to have access to this kind of data was strong. Their rationale was simple: With this information management could punish those who were taking advantage of the company. The order was given and the reports started getting generated.

As individuals began to be reprimanded based on the data, employees came to abhor the entire card key system. Upset with the Big Brother tactics, several employees figured out ways to enter and exit buildings without using their card keys—in effect rendering the whole safety component of the system useless.

In many organizations, it is striking just how suspicious employees are of information-related technology. The Information Age has truly helped shape the potential of organizations in ways that were unthinkable twenty years ago. It is possible today for an employee to know, with the touch of a keystroke, up-to-the-minute output and quality performance of an entire plant; the number of sales being generated on any given day; or the results of the most recent customer survey. This has extraordinary implications for teams and their vast potential as structures to quickly and effectively address a multitude of business issues. Yet it is the dark side of these new information capabilities that are often being exploited. Schemes to monitor how long employees are at their computer terminal, how many long-distance calls are made and to what numbers, or even what is being said during phone conversations are just a few examples of the dark side of this technology.

INFORMATION PHILOSOPHY

To create a HPWS, a very specific philosophy toward information sharing must be adopted. This philosophy has two essential elements:

1. There must be a widespread, open flow of information.
2. Information technology must be used in a responsible manner.

First, information must be seen as a right for everyone and not a privilege for a few. To the greatest extent possible, all information relevant to the performance of the company and to the performance of operations should be shared with employees. There must be a clear transition from divvying out information on a "need to know" basis to creating systems based on the fundamental assumption that employees have a "right to know."

Second, information technology must be used in a responsible manner that promotes and enhances team problem solving and decision making, not in ways that perpetuate suspicion of Big Brother monitoring. Douglas McGregor, in his watershed book *The Human Side of Enterprise,* postulated—over three decades ago now—that our fundamental assumptions about human nature would dramatically affect the systems and structures we devise in organizations. If we believe people are inherently active, want to do a good job, and tend to be self-motivated (McGregor's theory Y), we would never even consider listening in on a phone call or making employees punch a time clock. Since we assume employees are doing their best, it would be utterly unnecessary to monitor them. Conversely, if our assumptions hold that people are generally lazy, could care less about work, and completely lack any semblance of self-motivation (theory X), we would naturally use monitoring devices as a way to keep tabs on individuals. To create high performing teams, the workplace must be viewed from the perspective of theory Y—period. To do otherwise is to promote an aura of distrust within the organization that will work against the development of the team and their acceptance of information technology.

THE INFORMATION TRANSFER

Altering the way information flows requires a strong commitment by management since it is, in effect, shifting the very power structure of the organization—those who have greater access to information ultimately have greater influence on determining organizational outcomes. This commitment can be demonstrated by first making *contextual* information about the business easily accessible. This gives employees a broader perspective about the business, how it is performing, and the strategies that are being pursued to help improve its performance. The second stage of the transfer requires increasing the *operational* information that is available on the shop floor, at the customer service counter, or in the professional offices. People need to know relevant information regarding such things as quality, productivity, schedule, service, customer feedback, and product defects. Once these sources of information are made available, people will naturally begin identifying ways to improve the performance of their group. This requires a *feedback loop* so ideas are thoughtfully considered and, if they have merit, implemented.

On a macro level, the information transfer follows a path from the general to the specific:

Contextual
Operational
Feedback

THE BUSINESS CONTEXT

Rethinking the way the information is disseminated in the organization is a critical step in creating an empowered work force. Earlier we examined several examples of leaders who "told all" to their employees even as their peers denounced their actions as "dangerous." Tektronix's Fred Hanson started out with monthly assemblies during which the profit-and-loss statement and key strategies were openly presented to all the employees in his division. IBM's Bill Etherington crossed the entirety of Canada, speaking before hundreds of groups to explain what Transition '92 meant and how the new IBM would operate. Steelcase's Frank Merlotti went on a similar quest, zigzagging across the U.S. in an attempt to speak before every single employee in order to explain why teams were essential for the company's long-term survival. John Adamoli of Martin Marietta used a combination of regular assemblies and informal breakfast gatherings to communicate his message regarding the challenges facing the company. In the same vein, but with a different style and technology, Microsoft's Bill Gates sends out memos on the company's electronic mail system—accessible to all employees—describing his perspectives on the conditions facing the business.

In each of these cases, leadership took a central role in sharing information about the context of the business. And while each of these examples is of a senior-level manager, informing employees about the context of the business can just as easily come from a division GM, a plant manager, or even a team leader. What is critical is that all employees have clear access to information regarding the conditions facing the business, including:

- *Business mission.* The mission of the organization. Guiding values and principles. Operational guidelines/accepted norms of behavior.
- *Products and/or services.* What products/services the business provides to its customers. What differentiates the products in the marketplace.
- *Customers.* Who the customers are. What the customers desire from the product/service.
- *Performance measures.* The profit-and-loss statement of the company/division/plant. Performance against key business measures (e.g., output, quality, service level, inventory turns, customer satisfaction, etc.).
- *Competition.* Who the competition is. What differentiates their products/services in the marketplace. Strategies they are likely to pursue.
- *Strategy.* Current business strategy and business direction.

By helping employees understand the context of the business, the seeds of commitment are planted. If this information is considered "too important" to be openly shared, then neither strong commitment nor high performance can possibly be attained. At the root of a HPWS are employees who feel and act like partners—who genuinely feel a vested interest in the success or failure of the organization. This can be developed only if employees are informed extensively about the condition of the business.

It is also important to recognize that these business conditions are continually changing. Last year's presentation on competitors or last quarter's financial results will have little to do with the competitive position or financial performance in the coming year. As a guideline, business context information needs to be presented, at a minimum, every quarter. In most HPWSs, it is conveyed through assemblies at the end of each month. Through the effective use of information technology, it is possible to provide easy access on a daily or even hourly basis. The point is that the business context must be regularly and openly communicated.

OPERATIONAL PERFORMANCE

Once an ongoing means by which to communicate the context of the business has been established, the next step is to make specific, operational information available. This information is targeted at the job level. The intent is to provide employees with visibility of the performance of their work unit.

In their quest to create "a different kind of company," United Auto Workers (UAW) and General Motors officials agreed that *who had access to what kind of information* needed to be a central consideration in the design of the new Saturn Division. They determined jointly that only by providing specific, operational information to work teams—relating to everything from quality to output to cost—could the division's audacious goals be achieved. By making this kind of information widely available, Saturn developed an information-sharing design that was without precedent in the U.S. automobile industry. The benefits were recognized immediately: It gave teams the opportunity to identify cost and quality problems that would have otherwise remained invisible—in all likelihood, housed in neatly stacked reports in faraway offices. To reinforce the importance of applying this knowledge, production teams were put in charge—among other things—of developing and managing the budget for their work area. As the UAW's Joseph Rypkowski notes, "We've broadened the scope of their responsibility so they have a better and bigger picture of what it takes to run the business . . . they gain a better appreciation for what the organization has to do and what it costs in dollars."[1]

Operational information, like contextual information, has historically been concentrated in the hands of management or professional organizations—often to the detriment of the organization's overall performance. A former Hewlett-Packard executive is fond of telling a story about a process engineering group he managed that had been working on a difficult quality problem for weeks. One day a manufacturing operator accidentally wandered into the engineering offices and noticed the process-control charts the engineers were using to monitor the yield rates on the troubled assembly line. The operator took one look at the charts and immediately deduced what the problem was and why it was occurring. "As astonishing as it may seem," noted the executive, "it never occurred to us to show our data to the operators on the line until that exact moment when she showed us all up with a simple explanation as to what was happening out there. After that we began sharing everything."

Depriving groups of key information results in several predictable consequences:

- People don't seem to care much about their work and feel little connection with the workplace.
- The concerns that people voice, and the issues foremost on their minds, have nothing to do with the organization's performance (e.g., "Why can't we have Pepsi instead of Coke in the vending machines?" "Can we get a salad bar in the cafeteria?" "Is being ten minutes late going to go down on record as being tardy?").

- People may feel so completely alienated from the work experience that they seek outlets that, in the extreme, are destructive to the organization (e.g., product sabotage, unprofessional behavior).
- Problem solving tends to be unfocused, haphazard, and ineffective.

Operational information can be as crude as notes on a flip chart that serve as a communication linkage between work shifts or as elaborate as an electronic mail system that allows immediate feedback on pricing proposals from all over the world. The bottom line is simple: Operational information is the lifeblood of a high performing team. Without a substantive foundation of relevant business and operational information, performance is drastically impaired.

At a minimum, operational information must describe:

1. What is happening in the work unit (e.g., quality and output measures, the number of customer complaints, the latest status of a new product, any changes in direction based on new demands from customers)
2. The relationship between the work unit's performance and the overall objectives for the company
3. What the desires of the work unit's customers are and the degree to which those desires are being met
4. Direct feedback to team members relating to the performance of the work

INFO SUPERSHOCK

In most organizations opening up the communication channel is a central challenge, but there are exceptions. A new-product development team at Fisher Controls found themselves on so many distribution lists that the majority of their time was spent reviewing memos and other raw data that showed up in their E-mail file.

A frustrated team member observed, "We just can't assimilate it anymore—info passing is so easy, we're getting bombarded with everything, even when its relevance to us is questionable." The team became so flooded with data it began acting as if it were in a state of shock, unable to use its vast reservoir of information for any clear purpose. More and more teams are suffering from the malady of information supershock—particularly in organizations that are using advanced information technology to instantly convey countless tomes of data. The team simply receives so much information that it becomes impossible to interpret and effectively use it.

In many ways, information supershock is a more favorable problem than information deprivation, for it does suggest that the necessary infrastructure to channel information to the team is in place. The team is in a position to identify the information it needs in order to achieve its objectives. In helping to make this determination, a core HPWS design principle comes into play known as *minimum critical specification*. In this context, the question posed to the team becomes, "What is the absolute minimum information you need to successfully meet your objectives?" Any information that goes beyond this minimum set is not critical and, therefore, can be eliminated from consideration and review. Ironically, in going through this type of assessment, many teams discover that the minimum critical information they need is not contained in the volumes of data they are currently receiving. By targeting the *minimum critical,* they can identify what their real information needs are and where they can be found.

Regardless of whether the team is suffering from info supershock or info deprivation, the following five-step process is helpful:

1. Given the current context of the business, identify what the minimum critical information is for effective team performance.

2. Determine whether the needed information is currently being generated and is accessible.
3. Seek out the source of the information or define a process through which the needed information can be generated.
4. Use the information as a tool to characterize the team's current processes and level of performance.
5. Continually review the team's information needs and, as necessary, seek out sources to address information needs that arise.

The demands for information at the work team level are significantly greater in HPWSs than in traditionally designed organizations. This does not mean, however, that organizations need to hire a barrage of new support personnel whose role is to generate information for the newly forming teams. In fact, most of the information critical to team performance already resides inside most organizations. *The problem is not whether the information exists, but where the information goes.* Rather than having it follow a vertical path upward, it must be rechanneled to follow a horizontal path across the organization. And as teams more clearly define their minimum critical information needs, an intriguing irony often results—there is more consolidation of data and fewer lengthy reports. As information becomes used in a more focused way, much of the excess data collection becomes exposed and eliminated. As a manufacturing manager at Tektronix observed, "I receive a report of nearly five hundred pages each month—far too much to really understand or interpret. Of the five hundred-odd pages, three are critical to my team. Those three pages, in turn, could all be consolidated onto a single page. Now, imagine I go forward with a specific proposal to change the reporting from five hundred pages to one each month. Who do you think will be most opposed to my recommendation?"

He did make the recommendation and a group of eleven—who

generated the lengthy reports each month—was disbanded. This points out an important fact: By targeting what is critical, not only is the information the team receives more focused and useful, it may actually require *less support* and, correspondingly, *less cost* to generate.

THE FEEDBACK LOOP

Michelangelo is purported to have said that his role as an artist was not to create sculptures with his chisel and hammer but, rather, to release the figure that already existed inside the raw slab of stone. In a similar vein, once an information channel is established, the challenge is to unleash the problem-solving potential that already exists within the team.

The natural evolution of increased information availability is increased problem solving: The more an individual knows about the business and the operation of her work area, the more she is able to contribute in terms of identifying problems and suggesting alternatives for their resolution. It is important that as the amount and relevancy of information increase, it is complemented by a platform where employees can voice their views on the issues and problems that the new flow of information has suddenly made visible to them. The platform can be as simple as initiating regular meetings whose sole purpose is problem solving.

Initially, teams will be primarily focused on problem identification and on making recommendations for solutions. In effect, they are characterizing problems so that someone else can go out and fix them. Within a short period, there needs to be a shift so the teams are beginning to take primary responsibility for not only identifying problems and developing alternative solutions, but for managing the actual implementation of the solution.

To help teams make this important transition, management

FIGURE 14: Hierarchy of Problem-Solving Involvement

High Involvement

Ownership

Team is directly responsible for all aspects of problem solving and implementation of solutions (i.e., identification, recommendations of alternative solutions, and responsibility for assuring that the problem is "designed out" of the process). The team addresses problems relating to the performance of their work as well as competitive, organizational, and customer-related issues.

Resolution

Team is directly responsible for identifying and implementing solutions to the problems they encounter in their work area.

Recommendations

Group makes recommendations to management for possible solutions relating to problems they encounter in their work area.

Identification

Group is asked to identify problems in their work area. Any solutions that are developed or any actions taken are solely the responsibility of management.

Low Involvement

needs to take an active role in developing the team. This development effort includes providing teams with the necessary training, support, and coaching to:

- Clearly define the team charter—the team must have a well-defined purpose.

- Develop meeting skills.
- Begin effectively utilizing a problem-solving methodology.
- Utilize several different problem-solving tools and recognize the types of problems each is most helpful in addressing (e.g., cause-and-effect diagrams, Pareto, variance analysis, force-field analysis).
- Develop facilitation skills among the team's entire membership.
- Create operating guidelines for the team.
- Utilize action planning to clarify *who* is responsible for achieving *what* by *when*.

FEEDBACK GIMMICKRY

To create a HPWS, the very nature of the organization must undergo change. This is why there is such great emphasis on empowering people at the team level—at the very point where the work is being performed. Approaches that create parallel organizations (like quality circles) or parallel processes (like suggestion boxes or individual achievement awards) are often ineffective at creating sustained change in the way the organization operates. The focus needs to be on altering the way the dominant structure and systems operate—parallel organizations and processes do very little, and often damage efforts to achieve that end.

Spurred by reports of Toyota's remarkable success with suggestion boxes, North American and European companies began implementing them in droves during the early Eighties. It was cheap (all you needed was a box, an evaluation committee, and a small amount of money budgeted for cash payouts), easy (it didn't change any existing systems, structures, or roles), virtually risk-free (no need for damage control if it failed), and the potential payoff appeared to be great.

Today many companies have abandoned their suggestion boxes. In organizations where the boxes have remained, the results are, for the most part, unimpressive. The problem with suggestion boxes and other gimmickry (like Employee of the Month or individual achievement awards) are fourfold:

1. They do nothing to alter the core structures, systems, or processes of the organization.

While it is arguable that suggestion boxes are a form of participative management, they are, at best, a very primitive form. The fact is suggestion boxes can be—and often are—implemented in organizations that are extremely autocratic and antiparticipative in their philosophy, systems, processes, structures, and roles. These core elements remain completely unaffected by putting a suggestion box system or achievement awards in place.

2. They reward individuals often to the detriment of other individuals and teams.

Because most systems are designed to reward individuals for their ideas, there is absolutely no incentive to share ideas with other group members. If a good idea is shared in a group setting, the incentive is to be the first individual to write it out as a suggestion and turn it in. Often the originator of an idea is not the one who receives the cash payout. This perpetuates resentment and *idea secrecy*. Further, the ideas that are suggested tend to lack the refinement one would see if a team had generated and discussed it. As a result, many of the suggestions are poorly thought out, based on false assumptions, or trivial in nature.

3. Feedback takes far too long.

Feedback is most effective if it is immediate. Waiting days, weeks, or even months to hear if an idea has been accepted can hurt morale and decrease the likelihood that people will continue to make suggestions in the future.

4. It puts little or no responsibility on the person making the suggestion to implement it.

In this respect, there is no responsibility or accountability or even ownership for the suggestion. In the extreme, organizations have made payouts for ideas that were never implemented.

To demonstrate how ineffectual and ultimately absurd suggestion systems can become, consider the experience of an employee at a major aerospace company. Six weeks after turning in a suggestion, he received a letter from the Suggestion Committee. No, the letter did not explain why his idea was or was not going to be implemented. Rather, the letter informed him that his suggestion had been received by the committee and that it had been assigned a number. For any inquiries about the status of his suggestion in the future, he needed to refer to this tracking number. Six months later, he did inquire about the status of his suggestion. The committee informed him that they had not yet evaluated it but hoped to do so in the near future.

To achieve high performance, teams must ultimately be empowered to identify problems, make recommendations, come up with practical solutions, and take ownership for implementation. This is a huge shift from suggestion systems, which are based on the premise that management will receive recommendations and then determine whether the recommendations are worthwhile. The shift is so large, in fact, that during the transition to HPWSs, suggestion systems should be discontinued—the odds are the continued use of them will serve to stunt the development of the team as an effective improvement-generating unit.

RIGHT TO KNOW

The information transfer is about getting teams the data they need to take on increasing amounts of responsibility, accountability, and ownership for the performance of the business. Historically, information has been narrowly held, a jewel among those who have it, and divvied out strictly on a "need to know" basis. In the future, information must become a commodity, with open access to pertinent information the rule, as people within the organization are seen as having an inherent "right to know" about the performance of the business.

High performance teams must have timely and accurate contextual and operational information, for it is this information that both encourages and enables team problem solving. The information transfer requires the active participation of management in first rechanneling the way information is disseminated and then in helping develop the team's capability to effectively utilize it.

CHAPTER **10**

The New Agents
of Design

Many managers gasp at the prospect of delegating work design responsibility to the people who work for them. Teams, however, tend to develop designs that are comparable to those produced by industrial engineers or efficiency experts. It has been found that with some education and guidance, work teams will develop designs 85 to 90 percent congruent with the best work of outside experts and, perhaps even more important, they will be far more committed to the designs they create.[1] As Alvin Allison, a mechanic at Monsanto's Greenwood, South Carolina, plant points out, "I knew twenty years ago that I could direct my own job, but nobody wanted to hear what I had to say."[2] Now people are listening at Greenwood and the results have been impressive.

In the high performing organization, the new agents of design are the members of the team, collectively drawing on the expertise and wisdom of the group to develop new solutions to work design issues. Outside experts can add value to this effort by helping educate team members on the many intricacies of the redesign process, but it is ultimately the team that is responsible for the continuous design and redesign of work.

For teams to be effective in this role, several conditions must first be met:

1. The information infrastructure must be in place.

Information is the foundation on which any work design effort ultimately stands. A group lacking knowledge about business performance, customers, technology, and current operational effectiveness will, with certainty, develop a flawed design. Get the information infrastructure in place before charging the team with redesign responsibilities.

2. Teams must be given clear expectations and boundary conditions with regard to the redesign effort.

Expectations describe the desired outcomes for the redesign project while boundary conditions outline the specific constraints or limitations the team must consider. They are powerful tools for both maximizing the degree of team autonomy and minimizing the degree of risk to the organization.

3. Teams must be given legitimate authority and responsibility for work design.

While this seems an obvious point, the implication is often a difficult one for managers to swallow. Many groups are put "in charge" of work redesign efforts, but it is often little more than a mental exercise—the decision whether to implement the design still rests exclusively with management. Management must legitimize the effort up front and make a commitment to support the team's design.

4. Teams must have a basic understanding of work redesign methodologies.

This condition is particularly important. Getting teams involved in figuring out ways to improve their performance through developing more effective work designs is not a simple task. In fact, there can be a huge education and time commitment in getting team members to the point where they can effectively utilize the tools necessary to implement a redesign.

5. *Continual learning must be the centerpiece of the overall organization design.*

The life-sustaining force of continual improvement is continual learning—if a group is prevented from applying what they have learned to improve systems, processes, and procedures, continual improvement will quickly cease. High performing organizations are not stationary, stagnant, or finished—they are continually evolving as new ideas and new business conditions unfold. In this sense, no design is ever complete—it is, rather, the best effort to address present requirements given the team's current level of knowledge. Every design effort is ultimately destined for obsolescence as new learning broadens the team's knowledge and capability.

A STUDY IN REDESIGN: RISKY BUSINESS

How do these five points play out in actual redesign efforts? The following story describes how a manufacturing manager initiated a successful redesign effort in his organization.

While serving as the manufacturing manager of the Portable Instrument Division at Tektronix, Joe Burger wanted to get his manufacturing teams directly involved in relaying out the production line. His instincts told him they could develop a work flow superior to that of the industrial engineering group, and he wanted to gain their ongoing involvement in continually improving the performance of the assembly line. The open information sharing and work team training Burger had initiated over the last year had developed strong decision-making and problem-solving capability among the manufacturing employees. It was now time to take the effort to the next level of involvement.

Burger's staff showed little reaction when he announced his plan. A few days later he stated his expectations and boundary conditions to a task force with representatives from each of the manufacturing teams. A short training program, focused on work redesign methods, followed. Then the group started working on a new design.

The initial reports Burger received were very positive—people were clearly excited about the project. But as the completion deadline neared, several managers came to him with grave concerns. "Joe, the layout they've created will never work!" declared one manager.

When Burger first saw the plan he, too, noticed several flaws—flaws that would undoubtedly cripple the line's effectiveness. This put him in a dilemma: Was it better to take control of the project and make the changes necessary to get the design right and run the risk of alienating the members of the design team? Or was it better to accept and support the design—after all, they had met all his boundary conditions—and use it as a learning experience to improve the team's effectiveness on the next redesign effort? In the end, much to the dismay of several members of his staff, Burger chose the latter approach.

After a couple of weeks, the inherent flaws in the design had become readily apparent—the line balance was uneven and extra material handling was being required because of the physical location of several work stations. One day several members of the design team came to Burger asking him if they could have another shot at the design of the production line. Burger agreed and then watched in amazement as they quickly reformed, added some new members to the group, and set off to create a new design. A few days later it was complete.

The new design was phenomenal—it not only addressed the flaws from their first effort, it "designed out" several nagging problems assemblers had been dealing with for years. The design was so good, in fact, that line balancing became easy and material handling was dramatically reduced. Reductions in output time and increases in quality soon followed. Members of Burger's management team openly admitted that the design went well beyond anything they had ever conceived.

BEYOND THE "TECHNICAL IMPERATIVE"

Historically, work design has been based on a "technical imperative"—once the most efficient and effective means for utilizing a particular technology is determined, people are "force fit" into jobs. The technology-buying binge of General Motors in the mid-Eighties, when the company spent billions of dollars to automate the workplace in hope of lessening its reliance on human capital, dramatically illustrates the point. GM, largely ignoring the human side of the work design equation (with a few notable exceptions, such as the creation of the Saturn Division), embarked on what was perhaps the largest, most expensive redesign effort in history. The resulting factories were highly automated but operated by workers who, for the most part, were disenfranchised with the company.

Ford, by contrast, took a more balanced approach, emphasizing the development of work teams and increased employee involvement as paramount before making any decisions relating to the purchase of advanced technology. As Peter Pestillo, the Ford executive vice president who heads labor relations, noted, "GM was determined to minimize the role of the hourly people. Our goal was to maximize the contribution of the hourly people."[3]

In the end, Ford spent a fraction of what GM did on automation, but was able to achieve—as of 1992—a $795-per-vehicle price advantage over GM (the result of Ford's needing one-third fewer person hours to build its cars). Much of what Ford did was break down long-standing barriers between union and management—barriers that had previously limited meaningful involvement in problem solving and idea sharing among workers.

They, in effect, focused as much on issues relating to work roles, responsibilities, and employee involvement—all human or social-related issues—as they did on examining technical ones. This illustrates an important point: Work design based on the technical imperative is woefully inadequate and almost certainly assures the underutilization of human potential within the organization.

INITIATING THE REDESIGN

Before a redesign can be initiated, a decision must be made as to which redesign approach will be most appropriate. There are two commonly used approaches, each with different strengths and weaknesses:

1. *Top-down.* A design team, representing the entire organization, is formed. This team is responsible for the redesign of the total organization.
2. *Bottom-up.* Current or natural work groups are trained in the mechanics of redesign and begin improving their immediate work area. As design issues between groups surface, representative task forces are formed to address them.

REDESIGNING TOP-DOWN

The first step in this approach is to establish a design team. The design team is usually made up of a representative cross section of the organization. It is responsible for the complete redesign of the entire operation, including determination of equipment placement, process flow, work roles—even the compensation structure. This group often spends months—in some cases years—learning about HPWSs, becoming educated in work redesign methods, and analyzing the current operation before coming out with its redesign recommendations.

The greatest strength of this approach is that the total system is analyzed—not just a single work group or department. In this respect, the designs developed by the design team tend to be very good and highly effective. Further, if the members of the design team do a good job of getting the ideas of the people they represent heard and reflected in the work design that is ultimately created, there is generally a strong level of support for it.

The weakness of using a design team approach is twofold:

1. It is time- and resource-intensive.
2. The organization gets little, if any, immediate benefit—in the short term, in fact, performance declines are likely as people are pulled out to work as full-time members of the design team.

Numerous organizations have effectively used design teams in their redesign efforts. This has been a particularly effective approach in new plant start-ups (like Digital's Enfield, Connecticut, plant and Procter & Gamble's Lima, Ohio, plant).

REDESIGNING BOTTOM-UP

An alternative method—the bottom-up or natural work groups approach—has been used in a number of successful transitions of preexisting organizations (including efforts at Monsanto, Kodak, Tektronix, and IBM). In contrast to forming a single, representative design team, all employees become involved in the redesign process by helping improve the effectiveness of their current or natural work group.

The concept behind this approach is that as you improve the performance of the existing work groups, interface issues will become more evident and more urgent. A natural pull is then created for the formation of task forces to address these cross-team and cross-functional issues. Implemented effectively, the benefit of this approach is twofold:

1. There is nearly immediate improvement at the work group level.
2. The resistance to address cross-team and cross-functional issues is lessened since awareness of the negative effect of such issues is heightened.

In the natural work group approach, it is the work group that receives training and then immediately applies what they learn to their current work situation. There is no master, total organization work redesign—rather, it is more of an opportunistic strategy where barriers are identified as they emerge and are then eliminated. The end result is a complete redesign—just as it is with the design team approach—but the means is to address small pieces of the organization and not the entire system all at once.

The weakness of this approach is obvious: Since the focus is on only a part of the total system, it's possible to maximize the effectiveness of a natural work group while negatively affecting the overall performance of the organization. Second, this approach typically requires a significant training effort across the

FIGURE 15: Redesigning Top-Down vs. Bottom-Up

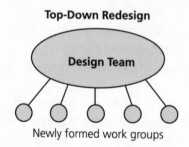

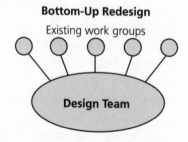

A design team, representing the entire organization, is formed. This team is responsible for the redesign of the total organization.

Current or natural work groups are trained in the mechanics of redesign and begin improving the immediate work area. As design issues between groups surface, representative task forces are formed to address them.

organization on the front end, so it, like the design team approach, can be time-, money-, and resource-consuming. Finally, this approach requires a strong commitment by management to help the teams eliminate barriers.

Is one approach superior to the other? No. Each has certain strengths and weaknesses. In general, the design team approach works best when there is *not* a strong vested interest in maintaining current structures or processes. This approach works well in new plant start-ups where there is no existing hierarchy or departmental structures. In contrast, using natural work groups tends to be more effective in redesigning an existing organization.

THE MECHANICS OF REDESIGN

Regardless of the approach, teams cannot simply be "turned loose" and expected to become effective agents of design. They must follow a disciplined process that examines business conditions, technology, and human issues. This point is sometimes lost on managers who "want to do the right thing" by quickly turning over design responsibilities to their group. Turning over responsibility for redesigning work flow, processes, and roles without supporting it through training, experience, information, and knowledge is actually a form of management abdication. Teams—whether they are in a manufacturing, sales, service, or executive setting—need to understand the mechanics of redesign.

Open-systems theory, which first emerged in the 1950s, is the core framework for designing organizations for high performance. In its most simplistic form, the theory suggests that the survival of an organization is dependent on its ability to continually adapt to changes in its external environment. Failure to adapt to changes, whether they are technical, market, regulation, or even demographic driven, will mean the eventual extinction of the enterprise. An example is the shakeout that occurred among the mechanical-calculator companies when electronic technology enabled consumers to purchase the cheaper, smaller, more fully featured calculators. It no longer mattered which company built the best mechanical calculator because the entire market had been replaced by a new technology. Only those companies that were leading the change, or able to see the potential impact of the new technology and quickly adapt, survived. The same was true of the buggy whip manufacturers with the coming of the automobile and of the Swiss watch manufacturers with the coming of the quartz-movement watch. These examples are extreme, but each amplifies a significant point: An organization's survival is dependent on its ability to respond to ever-changing conditions from its external environment.

THE LIFE-SUSTAINING CYCLE

The life-sustaining cycle of organizations consists of four basic elements: input, transform, output, and feedback. Examples of *input* would include capital, raw materials, component parts, new hires, and information. Input is literally anything that is brought into the organization. Once inside, these inputs are *transformed* or altered in some manner. Raw material is transformed into a product; a telephone call is transformed into an order; a new hire is transformed into a value-adding employee. Next, an *output* emerges—prime examples would include a finished product or completed service. The outputs are what the organization actually sells to its customers (whether these are services or products). In the final step, the organization receives *feedback* relating to its products/services from a variety of sources (e.g., government—the product doesn't meet Federal safety standards; customers—the response to a new service offering is highly favorable). The feedback may point out the requirement for ongoing changes, redesign, and adaptation on the part of the organization. The

FIGURE 16: Open-Systems Model

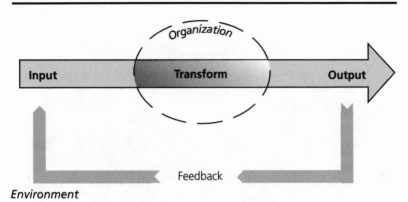

Environment

organization's ultimate success is completely dependent on how well it sustains its input-transform-output-feedback cycle under ever-changing business conditions.

THE BUSINESS CONDITIONS SCAN

When involved in a work redesign effort, it is critical to consider the open-systems model. Consistent with the model, the first step in a redesign effort is a scan of the current environment facing the business. A thorough scan encompasses an assessment of factors such as:

CUSTOMERS/MARKETS
- Who are your major customers?
- What are the major markets you serve?
- What are the expectations of customers today? What are they likely to be three to five years from now? In what ways are customer desires changing?

FIGURE 17: Environmental Globe

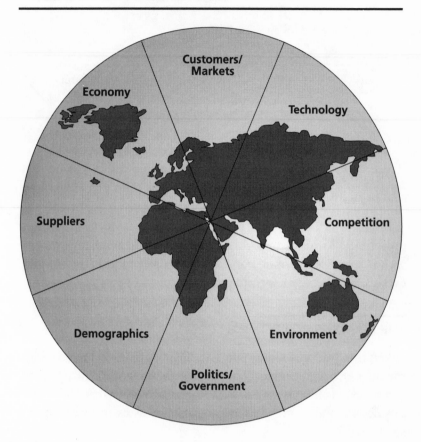

TECHNOLOGY
- What technologies do you need that you currently do not have? In what ways will these technologies increase your performance/quality/price/delivery/service?
- How effective is the team at integrating new technologies into the current operation? How could it be made more effective?

COMPETITION

- In what ways has your competition changed in the last several years?
- What are the key features of your competition's products/services that differentiate them from yours?

ENVIRONMENT

- What are the current trends in environmental protection that will likely impact your team well into the future? What changes/improvements can you make now in preparing for the future?
- How sensitive are people in your organization toward environmental issues? In what ways could their awareness of environmental issues be increased?

POLITICS/GOVERNMENT

- What major domestic and world events are impacting your team? What are specific examples of that impact?
- Are there imminent government regulations that will have a likely impact on the organization? What will be the effect? How can the organization prepare for these changes?

DEMOGRAPHICS

- Are you able to hire and retain top-caliber talent? Why?
- Do women and minorities get fair advancement opportunities? How could this be improved?
- In what ways have you adjusted workplace arrangements to be consistent with the changing makeup of the work force? (e.g., "cafeteria-style" benefit packages? Flexible time off? Child care?)

SUPPLIERS

- Who are your primary suppliers? How good is your working relationship with them? How aware are they of the processes utilized by your team?
- How much opportunity do team members have to interface

with suppliers? Would enhanced communication be helpful? How could this be accomplished?

ECONOMY

- What would be the likely effects of a downturn in the economy on your team? How could the negative impact of such a downturn be minimized?
- To what extent is the business affected by currency fluctuations, inflation, interest rates, etc.? What is the impact on your team?

Often it is helpful to begin the environmental scan by using a survey instrument to narrow down the factors that are most likely to have a direct effect on the organization. Once the critical factors are identified, a more in-depth and detailed analysis of their likely impact and strategies for dealing with them can be developed. The results of this type of scan can be powerful. One assessment, done by a production group in a high-tech firm, concluded that the sophistication of the technology used on future products was likely to be well beyond the current knowledge base of its technical staff. To combat the impeding technical obsolescence, an extensive education program—including the sponsorship of individuals seeking electronic engineering degrees—was introduced.

THE INNER-WORKINGS ANALYSIS

Once an understanding of the conditions facing the organization has been developed, the focus of the redesign effort turns to the internal workings of the team. How well, given the current conditions it faces, does the team transform inputs to outputs? What areas could be improved? In doing this assessment it is helpful to examine the technical system (work flow, processes, technologies, equipment) and social system (people, culture, leadership, reporting structures, rewards). The extent to which these two systems are aligned with the realities and opportunities of current business conditions, the greater the success the organization will ultimately enjoy.

There is a variety of methods for conducting assessments of existing technical and social systems. The outcome of this analysis is an understanding of the strengths and weaknesses of the current work design. Some of the specific, and more common, methods used in this analysis include:

Variance Analysis

This method requires that all of the variances or problems that can occur at each step in a given process are identified and listed in order of occurrence. In a manufacturing setting this might include such things as the wrong type of material being delivered or the wrong part being installed. In a service setting it could be an incorrect order entry or the failure to track a potential customer. The intended outcome of the analysis is twofold. First, a control chart is created that identifies the origin of all variances. By pinpointing where variances first appear, the team can then work toward eliminating them entirely or, at the very least, controlling them at the source of occurrence.

Second, the analysis helps identify where a lack of information and the ineffective coordination of efforts are contributing to variances. In considering this data for redesign, the implications often include expanded work roles and the realignment of departments.

Value-Adding Analysis

This methodology also requires a thorough examination of the current work process. But rather than looking for variances, the focus is on uncovering recurring activities that are of a non-value-adding nature. In this framework, non-value-adding is any activity that introduces waste (e.g., wasted time, wasted energy, wasted quality) into the work flow. Once non-value-adding activities are identified, plans can be developed for eliminating them.

Often, much of the "waste" uncovered by this analysis relates to where decision-making authority actually resides. One team discovered that the amount of time required to gain management approval for expenditures of less than two hundred dollars was sometimes several weeks. In another case, employees at a customer service desk noted the amount of wasted time and energy that resulted from a requirement that they get management approval before issuing refunds to customers. In both instances, the value-adding capability of the team was enhanced by changes to the "social system."

Process Re-Engineering

Process re-engineering, as its name suggests, puts the overall process or work flow at the centerpiece of the redesign effort. Current work flow is first charted and then ways to simplify or streamline it are evaluated. Particular attention is paid to bottlenecks and departmental boundaries that disrupt a smooth, uninterrupted flow of the process under evaluation.

Regardless of the methodology selected (and there are literally hundreds from which to choose), the desired outcome is to first examine how work is currently being performed within the organization. From such an assessment, obvious opportunities for improvement begin to emerge.

CREATING THE REDESIGN

At this stage in the process, the team has fully assessed three critical elements of the current work system. They have defined:

- Conditions facing the business that are likely to have a direct impact on their operation
- Current status of the technical system
- Current status of the social system

FIGURE 18: Principles of High-Performance Design

Control Design Principles	Commitment Design Principles
• *Local Optimum:* Energy is focused on how to maximize the performance of a subunit.	• *Global Optimum:* Energy is focused on how to maximize the performance of the entire organization.
• *Maximum Specification:* To the greatest extent possible, all aspects of jobs and methods are specified.	• *Minimum Critical Specification:* Only the most critical aspects of jobs and methods are specified.
• *Functional Defect Control:* Defects, if they cannot be eliminated, are controlled by a specialized function (e.g., quality-control inspector).	• *Source Defect Control:* Defects, if they cannot be eliminated, are controlled as near the point of origin as possible.
• *Specialized Skill:* Employees are highly specialized with a narrow skill set.	• *Multiskilled:* Employees are cross-trained, multiskilled, and highly flexible.
• *Vertical Information Flow:* Information goes up the management hierarchy.	• *Source Information Flow:* Information goes directly to the point where direct action can be taken.
• *Work Ethic Value:* A core organization value is that working hard is important.	• *Work Life Value:* A core organization value is to provide a high quality of work life.
• *Conservative Improvement:* The organization improves through a formal process of management carefully planning out and instituting policy and procedural and method changes.	• *Continuous Improvement:* The organization is continuously improving its performance through the redesign of work, experimentation, and risk taking.

The team is now ready to develop an initial redesign proposal. In developing the proposal, it is critical that the seven principles of high performance design be carefully considered. Each of these principles can have significant implications on how work flow, structures, processes, and roles are ultimately designed. These principles can be summarized as:

1. Global Optimum: Energy is focused on how to maximize the performance of the entire organization.

The "big picture" must always be taken into consideration whenever a job or function is being redesigned—the performance of a single team cannot be maximized at the expense of the overall performance of the organization. By going through a redesign process where the external factors affecting business and their implications on the work design are considered, resulting designs do tend to be more oriented toward the global, rather than the local, optimum.

To maintain the total organization perspective on an ongoing basis, it is helpful to have regular communication forums. At the Forest Grove circuit-board facility, the status of every order in the plant and the issues facing each sequence of the operation are reviewed daily by representatives from each work team. At Monsanto's Chocolate Bayou plant, the status of the plant's overall operation is immediately available via a computer terminal. In both instances, employees have a perspective of the total operation and a high level of awareness of how changes in their immediate work area could affect the performance of the plant.

2. Minimum Critical Specification: Only the most critical aspects of jobs and methods are specified.

Often management tries to dictate or specify nearly all aspects of jobs and methods through rigid policy and procedure manuals. The mistaken assumption is that through the enforcement of these narrowly defined rules and policies, management will ensure greater consistency and control over the operation. Ironically, the outcome is often quite the opposite. At Martin Marietta, managers once joked about "malicious compliance" as a strategy for stopping decisions with which they disagreed. "If you did everything by the book [followed all the governing rules, policies, and procedures], you could bring the organization to a halt in a matter of days," noted one manager. This very same strategy is sometimes used by unions during contract disputes. Minimum critical specification suggests that there should be as few rules, procedures, and policies as possible. By eliminating these needless barriers, on-the-job creativity and innovation are given far more room to flourish.

In applying the "minimum critical" principle, a team in Honeywell's Building Controls Division replaced a three-inch volume that documented their product-development procedures with a twenty-page guideline.[4] The leadership team at Monsanto's Ruabon, Wales, facility regularly nominates policies for elimination. In both cases the intent is the same—identify the critical policies, procedures, and rules that must be in place and eliminate the rest.

3. Source Defect Control: Defects, if they cannot be eliminated, are controlled as near the point of origin as possible.

The old practice of adding a quality-control station to "inspect quality in" is long gone. In fact, there is considerable evidence that by adding quality-control inspection stations, the overall quality of the product or service tends, over time, to decline. This principle states what the quality gurus have been saying for years— quality must be a shared responsibility of the entire organization, not the responsibility of a single department. In essence, those performing the work should have the necessary knowledge and tools to assure that the product or service they pass on to their customer is total quality. By integrating total-quality responsibility into the work teams at Northern Telecom's Morrisville,

North Carolina, plant, the number of full-time quality inspectors dropped 40 percent while overall quality improved by 50 percent.[5]

4. Multiskilled: Employees are multiskilled, knowledgeable about the business, and highly flexible.

It has become clear that there are tremendous advantages in having employees who are multiskilled and capable of performing a variety of jobs and functions. By having a multiskilled work force, disruptions due to absenteeism, changes in demand, and equipment failure can be more effectively and expediently addressed. Skill variety, one of the key job design attributes that cross-training promotes, has been found to be an important element in jobs that people find motivating and personally rewarding.

A concern often raised is that by emphasizing cross-training and the development of a multiskilled work force, aren't employees becoming "jacks of all trades and masters of none"? This is a legitimate concern. In fact, some jobs are complex, and it's often not practical to widely cross-train other team members due to the extensive amount of formal education or the advanced level of skill mastery required. All employees need to share certain core competencies, however, and in this regard all employees can be thought of as "cross-trained." These core competencies would include knowledge of:

- Customers
- Products/services
- Business performance
- Interpersonal skills (e.g., communication, giving and receiving feedback)
- Team effectiveness skills (e.g., decision making, effective meetings)

5. Source Information Flow: Information goes to the point where direct action can be taken.

Often the flow of information is designed to go up the management hierarchy to where decisions are made, and then back down to some lower level where they are actually implemented. This design principle suggests that the flow of information should take a different route: It should provide people, at all levels, with adequate information to make daily decisions on how to improve the performance of their work and solve problems that directly affect them.

6. Work Life Value: A core organization value is to provide a high quality of work life.

One of the emerging values of the last decade was the importance of a good quality of working life. The old adage "You only work for a paycheck" is not acceptable to most employees today—nor should it be acceptable to organization leaders. The workplace must be seen as an institution that fosters personal development, growth, education, and challenge. Ideally, the experience an individual has in the workplace helps her toward personal improvement in all aspects of her life.

Creating the sense of personal growth is an important design consideration that affects people beyond the boundaries of the workplace. At Cummins Engine, where HPWTs have been in place for a number of years, a team leader describes it this way: "The team concept has real meaning for them, not just as production operators but as human beings."[6]

7. Continuous Improvement: The organization is continuously improving its performance through the redesign of work, experimentation, and risk taking.

Continuous improvement requires a setting that encourages the free exchange of ideas and continuous experimentation. Since many innovations are the outgrowth of mistakes and initial failures, it is important that failures are evaluated in terms of what was learned rather than who should be punished.[7]

By using these principles as a guide, teams will develop designs that avoid some of the traditional traps, including:

- Tendency to focus on the effectiveness of individual groups or departments, often to the detriment of the organization's overall performance
- Developing communication pathways that greatly limit who has access to information
- Defining jobs that are narrow and lack challenge
- Underutilizing the creative and problem-solving potential of employees

ASSESSING THE REDESIGN

Once the design is implemented, there will invariably be problems. No design is perfect nor is any design ever truly complete. It is for this very reason that teams are so effective as agents of design—they can immediately recognize how the new work flow, structures, and roles help or hinder their ability to perform.

The redesign should be assessed on two levels. The level-one assessment examines how effective the design is at getting the team's product/service to its customers. Based on this evaluation, changes can be implemented to further improve the team's effectiveness. This process should be a continual, ongoing examination that leads to continual refinement of the design.

It is not uncommon for some teams to go through redesign efforts on a regular basis—often more than once a year. In the extreme, some teams actually redesign their work area on a weekly or even daily basis to meet shifts in product demand or configurations. In one instance, the regularity with which the team was changing the design of their area led them to put rollers on all the workbenches and tables so that the work flow could be more quickly redesigned as need dictated.

The second level of analysis examines the whole redesign process and attempts to answer the question "What was learned from this process that could improve redesign efforts in the future?" The intent is to catalog learning so that future redesign efforts can be accomplished with increasing rates of speed and effectiveness.

THE NEW AGENTS OF DESIGN

The redesign process outlined here is as appropriate with a six-member work team that is trying to improve its operating effectiveness as it is with a twenty-person design team that is trying to redesign a two-hundred-fifty-person division. The specific sequence of the steps is:

1. Conduct an environmental scan (assess such things as customers/markets, technology, competition, environment, politics/government, demographics, suppliers, economy).
2. Determine implications of the scan (based on the scan, determine which external conditions are likely to have a direct impact on the organization being analyzed).
3. Conduct a technical and social analysis (a variety of tools can be used, including a variance analysis, process reengineering, and value-added analysis to examine the existing design).
4. Initial redesign (assess the proposed design against the seven principles of HPWSs).
5. Implement redesign (try out the proposed design and uncover its strengths and weaknesses).
6. Apply lessons learned (catalog what was learned from the effort and incorporate the learning into future efforts).

The new agents of design are team members, not outside experts. To be effective in this role, teams need adequate information, clear expectations and boundary conditions, legitimate authority and responsibility for work design, an understanding of work design methodology, and the opportunity to assess what they have learned from their experiences. While "turning over" work design responsibility to teams will make many managers nervous—and some failures will likely ensue—it is a critical step in developing teams that are capable of sustaining high levels of performance.

CHAPTER 11

The Reinforcement Factor

Since Frederick Herzberg first cast doubt on the value of pay as a source of motivation back in the 1960s, the evidence to support his position has steadily grown. Yet pay and reward systems have remained in the forefront of many change efforts, cast there by an outdated ethic that suggests that only money can change behavior and drive up motivation. Conversely, some organization change efforts have ignored rewards altogether, the logic being, "If pay doesn't motivate, why worry about it?"

THE PAY PUZZLE

Just where does pay fit when attempting to transform an organization? First, pay is a critical issue to address—it simply cannot be sidestepped or ignored. In fact, as teams within the organization increase their levels of responsibility and authority, the murmur of dissatisfaction with the existing compensation structure will grow ever louder. Second, while pay will increasingly become an issue, it is almost always better addressed in the later stages of the transition, well after teams have been formally established and operational. Changes to the pay system should not—except under extraordinary circumstances—be used to initiate the transition to HPWS.

There are three factors supporting this position:

1. A tremendous amount of change can occur in the way information is disseminated and the way the work is designed without any dramatic changes to the formal reward structure.

Most people recognize the intrinsic benefits of HPWSs and have a genuine desire to help improve the performance of their organization. Studies of pay satisfaction show that it runs higher in companies stressing teamwork—even when the actual dollar amount received by employees is exactly the same as in companies without teams.[1] Focusing on pay too early in the transition can actually serve to distract efforts focused at developing team effectiveness.

2. It is difficult to develop a compensation system that truly reinforces work behaviors that are not yet present in the work area.

Without question, pay can influence behavior. This can be either positive or negative depending on the design of the compensation package. In developing a new system, it is often difficult to predict exactly what will be reinforced. Sears, in an attempt to boost sales in its automotive repair department, introduced a commission-based pay system for thousands of its employees. Sales did get an initial boost, but at the expense of customer trust. An eighteen-month undercover operation by the state of California found that the mechanics working under the incentive plan were charging an average of $223 for unnecessary car repairs. When the story broke, Sears auto centers immediately saw a 20 percent decline in business. At the height of the crisis, the company was hit with an estimated $700,000 a day in lost revenue.[2]

In efforts where compensation is used to "lead in" the change, the result is often a pay system that has little positive effect on team evolution. In the extreme, the pay system can serve to actually stunt team development. Employees who are "under an incentive" to be team players but who have neither the knowledge nor support to be effective in this new role are set up for failure.

K2 Skis, in an effort to improve quality, output, and teamwork, introduced a gain-sharing program at their manufacturing facility on Vashon Island in Washington State. The program consisted of five different components that employees could influence: (1) quality, (2) amount produced, (3) safety, (4) housekeeping, and (5) performance to schedule. Each component was weighted and measured on a regular basis. Despite what appeared to be a sound design, the system began to run into problems almost immediately. Because payouts were given based on individual and overall plant performance, differences in performance ratings among differing departments soon became an area of contention. A manufacturing delay in one department would sometimes be met with a barrage of criticism and anger. In some cases, bitter yelling matches between groups ensued.

To further worsen matters, a decline in ski sales—largely the result of the lingering recession and a year of particularly poor ski conditions throughout North America—left the company's profitability plummeting. This meant that even if significant manufacturing improvements were achieved, there would be no money available for the gain-sharing payout. Recognizing the insolvency of the program, employees became predictably disenfranchised and just a year after its introduction, gain sharing was abandoned at K2.

The unfortunate events at K2 left many in the organization with a bitter taste in regard to teams. Fortunately, K2 has battled back. Having experienced considerable improvements by using Just-in-Time manufacturing techniques, the organization is now heading down a path toward the implementation of high-performance teams. Other organizations, less responsive and flexible than K2, have been mired down for years after leading in with compensation packages that proved ineffective.

3. Compensation is a corporate "sacred cow" and typically among the most difficult systems to change.

This is a pragmatic consideration but one that change agents should heed. The compensation system is often protected by procedures and processes that are trying to assure equity in pay practices within the company and across the industry. In large companies this becomes a particularly important function of the compensation department. Sophisticated controls (such as narrowly focused job descriptions, the numerical valuing of jobs, and the use of pay surveys) are used to assure that the equity balance is maintained. Changes that require deviations from these mechanisms (such as "generic" job descriptions or skill-based pay schemes) are looked upon with great suspicion and apprehension. If it cannot be demonstrated that the nature of the work has changed, then there is typically little or no motivation from the corporate perspective to change the pay system. This "reality" clearly suggests the advantage in getting the other design changes in place first so a case for changing the compensation package can be made and supported.

While most companies have stringent policies that discourage or, in the extreme, make it virtually impossible to change the corporate compensation system, there are two notable exceptions: Weyerhaeuser and Monsanto. Within each of these companies individual plants can implement alternative pay and reward structures that are completely unique to their site. As Weyerhaeuser's human-resources manager Rick Nicholson notes, "They [the plants] are free to do whatever they think will be most effective for their business." Similarly, at the 1988 Monsanto Personnel Conference a paper was presented entitled "Alternate

Reward Strategies," which described compensation approaches ranging from pay for knowledge, to gain sharing, to lump-sum bonuses. The message at this landmark conference was very clear: The corporation will support any reward system that will help achieve superior results.

It is significant that within both Monsanto and Weyerhaeuser the use of alternative reward strategies is seen as a means to support and solidify other, fundamental changes to the plants. Leading an organization change effort with pay is discouraged. Rather, it is seen as a way to reinforce and enhance previous improvements.

THE COMPENSATION SAVIOR

Too often managers get caught up in the belief that a new compensation package will help them bound over other fundamental problems within the organization. "If people were paid differently, they'd work harder," is a common phrase echoing in the corridors by frustrated managers. The facts simply don't bear out this perspective. Compensation is not a savior—the "right" incentive system *will not* dramatically increase quality, output, customer service, or morale. It is arguable that the best compensation system that can ever be devised is one that upsets the fewest number of people within a given organization. Pay is not a source of sustained motivation. It is, rather, a defense against dissatisfaction.

LEADING WITH PAY

There are circumstances—albeit exceptional—when pay must be addressed early in the change effort. An assembly line at Tektronix, for example, had a piecework pay scheme in place—if a person stuffed components into circuit boards at a rate consistently higher than the average for the production line as a whole, then she would receive a performance bonus. This created a huge disincentive to share information or improvement ideas since helping other assemblers up their performance would raise the standard on which everyone's bonus payout was based. This pay system was designed in such direct opposition to teaming that it stood as an enormous barrier during the early stages of the transition to HPWTs.

In instances where the existing pay system provides a strong incentive *against teamwork*, an alternative design must be put in place during the earliest phases of the change effort. In a similar vein, if the existing compensation package is noncompetitive, leaving the organization with excessive turnover and other forms of employee dissatisfaction, then changes to the pay structure must again occur early in the transition. This was clearly the case at one firm which had a 40 percent turnover rate, largely due to low wages, in the manufacturing area. It simply made no sense to invest heavily in team development with their revolving-door turnover rate. Instead, the first issue to tackle was how to stabilize the work force and end the mass exodus. This required a new compensation package including higher, more competitive pay.

Only when the following two conditions exist is it appropriate to "lead" the change effort by restructuring the pay system:

- The existing system creates a strong incentive *against* teamwork.
- Noncompetitive pay practices have created an unstable work force.

These instances are clearly the exception. As a general rule, the redesign of the compensation should lag behind the more fundamental changes of establishing open communication linkages, chartering and developing teams, and redesigning work flow and processes.

DESIGNING THE PERFECT PAY SYSTEM

There is, of course, no such thing as the perfect pay system. In regard to HPWSs, there is not even a single best pay methodology. Ironically, this was not always thought to be true. Throughout the 1970s, most of the innovative plants (such as Procter & Gamble's Lima, Ohio, plant and Gaines Foods in Topeka, Kansas) were using skill-based pay. Skill-based pay promoted skill diversification and cross-training, necessary ingredients for assuring organization responsiveness and employee development. Because of the success of these firms, many began to equate high performance teams with skill-based pay practices—you simply could not have one without the other.

Today we know this is not the case—there are many innovative organizations that are using any one of a variety of different pay strategies. In fact, for many teams skill-based pay—which lends itself well to "choir teams" but poorly to "symphony teams"—may be completely inappropriate. While there are hundreds of variations, almost all of the compensation methods used with teams can fall into one of four categories:

- Gain sharing
- Profit Sharing
- Merit-Based
- Skill-Based

GAIN SHARING

Gain sharing is based on a very simple notion: The gains that employees help the company achieve are shared. Actually designing an effective program, however, is a complex and difficult undertaking. What, for example, should constitute a "gain"? Productivity? Quality? Time to market? Service level? Customer satisfaction? How will the dollar value of a gain in performance be

FIGURE 19: Pay Matrix

Plan Type	Description	Advantages	Disadvantages
Gain sharing	Monetary benefits of increased productivity, cost reductions, and improved quality shared with employees through regular cash bonuses.	• Enhances coordination and teamwork • Employees learn more about the business and focus on objectives • Reinforces participative work environments	• Company may have to pay bonus even when unprofitable • High administrative costs • Tends to be ineffective in large organizations
Profit sharing	Monetary benefits shared annually with employees in the form of cash, retirement, or a combination based on company profits.	• Incentive formula is simple—easy to communicate and understand • Firm pays only when profitable • Unites financial interests of owners and employees	• Lack of correlation between work effort and benefit • Tends to be ineffective in large organizations • Focus on short-term profit could have long-term consequences

Merit-Based

Salary or wage determined solely or largely by the employee's or group's performance.

- Effective if employees perceive relationship between pay and performance
- Can benefit company if measured performance correlates with team/company objectives

- Difficult to achieve trust in mgt.—employees may perceive system as unfair
- Most employees view their performance as above average—can demotivate
- Creates unhealthy competition between employees

Skill-Based

Salary or wage based on the number of skills the employee knows and can perform.

- Increases flexibility of company
- Company can operate with a leaner staff
- Increases employee incentive to expand depth and breadth of skills/knowledge
- Emphasizes importance of continual growth and development

- Raises labor costs as employees learn new skills
- False expectations due to lack of vacancies in areas of newly learned skills
- "Topping out"

calculated? How much of the gains will be shared with employees?

Since gain-sharing payouts are typically based on the performance of the team, unit, or division, team members are under an incentive to work together toward achieving the common goals of their organization. In this way, gain sharing helps promote cooperation and teamwork.

While there are numerous examples of highly successful gain-sharing plans, it remains true that many gain-sharing efforts outright fail. Among the most common reasons for failure include:

The formula for determining the gains is based on performance measurements the team cannot control.

This point is often overlooked. Frequently, the outcomes a team can realistically effect are exaggerated. This creates a negative dynamic that can cut two ways:

1. The team may be rewarded for performance it did nothing to help improve.
2. Or the team may be penalized for poor performance it did not effect.

In either case, the team develops a certain degree of cynicism toward the entire program. The massive gain-sharing program Du Pont's Fibers Unit attempted to introduce in the late Eighties fell prey to this trap. The program, which was touted by many as a bellwether event that would have far-reaching implications relating to compensation across the industry, was designed to pay employees a bonus based on the unit's performance against after-tax income goals. A sliding scale was devised where at less than 80 percent performance against plan, employees could lose up to a maximum of 6 percent of their salary. At 150 percent performance against plan, employees could receive a bonus of up to 12 percent of salary. Nearly eighteen thousand employees took part in the program.

The program began to falter when employees recognized that there were many factors affecting the unit's declining income that were beyond their immediate control—the ongoing worldwide recession, the increasing threat of war in the Middle East, and the continuing rise in oil prices were three pertinent and obvious examples. As performance against plan dropped further, to below the 80 percent level, frustrations mounted and the program was ultimately discontinued just two years after its initiation.[3]

The formula is not related to long-term business objectives or sustainable competitive advantage.

It is possible to develop a gain-sharing plan that gives big payouts for what is actually lackluster performance. This becomes especially true if the organization implementing the program does not have good benchmarking data with which to compare its current level of performance against that of its competitors or other top-performing companies in its industry. Without this information, it is possible to establish criteria that gives payouts based on improvements over historical performance rather than the level of improvement necessary to remain competitive.

The team does not have the opportunity and/or skills to problem-solve and implement performance-improvement ideas.

Numerous studies have come to the same conclusion that gain sharing works best in organizations where there is already a culture conducive to team participation and problem solving. In other words, gain sharing is not particularly effective at helping create teams. Rather, it is helpful in enhancing the performance of teams that already exist. Introducing a gain-sharing plan where management autocracy reigns is essentially futile. Teams need to be established and operating.

Experimentation with gain sharing has grown steadily in recent years, so much so that nearly 73 percent of existing gain-sharing programs have been implemented since 1980.[4] Part of the reason for the proliferation in interest is the number of team-based organizations that are emerging. Gain sharing is a natural incentive for team performance.

Gain sharing is also a fairly flexible method of pay—it can work as well in professional services organizations as it does in manufacturing operations. It remains true, however, that many of the efforts to implement gain sharing ultimately fail. Like all the various compensation practices described here, while the program itself is conceptually quite simple, the intricacies involved in successful implementation are remarkably complex.

PROFIT SHARING

Profit sharing is similar to gain sharing in that employees share directly in the gains they have helped achieve. In a typical profit-sharing program, a percentage of the company's profits are shared with all employees. At Tektronix, for example, 35 percent of all company profit was shared with employees. The amount actually received was calculated as a percentage of base salary. Through the years the bonus had been as high as 70 percent of base salary.

The advantage of profit sharing is that it focuses teams on the true bottom line—profitability. Further, it instills an ethic of sharing the company's wealth. This ethic of "sharing in the wealth we helped create" is highly conducive to teamwork. Finally, since profits are shared only when the organization is profitable, profit sharing avoids a potential problem many gain-sharing programs encounter: giving bonus payouts during periods when the organization is in the red.

Profit sharing is not exempt from problems, however. Among the most common:

People may see little connection between their actions and the company's profitability.

This becomes particularly true as the number of people in the program grows. Surprisingly, in organizations with as few as five hundred employees, people will begin to report that they don't really feel they can have much of a direct impact on profitability. In companies where thousands are on the same profit-sharing plan, employees see virtually no connection between the performance of their team and corporate profitability. In the extreme, profit sharing can even work against company cooperation as highly profitable divisions show their scorn toward the divisions who are "keeping our profit share down."

The program can become perceived as an entitlement.

This was so much the case at one firm, they actually adjusted their base-salary levels to 80 percent of what employees could get in the local market relying on profit sharing—which had historically run in the 25 to 30 percent range of base salary—to make up the difference. While recruiting new hires, the profit-sharing program was presented as the golden nugget: "Don't worry about a lower base salary. After profit sharing kicks in, you'll make more here than anywhere else in town." When the company's profitability declined, people were understandably upset. The money they had been *entitled* to was suddenly missing from their paychecks.

Profit sharing can serve as an incentive for short-term profit taking at long-term expense.

Often profitability has nothing to do with positioning the organization for longer-term success. Forgoing short-term profits in order to gain increased market share has been a common strategy among Japanese firms that sought expansion into North America. Delaying technology upgrades or postponing new hires in order to shore up profits can have negative repercussions well down the road. In some instances, the focus on profit has led teams to make trade-offs on quality and service that were clearly not in the best interest of the customer. Simply, creating an incentive for teams to put profit first may result in decisions that are not in the best interest of the firm.

Despite these potential pitfalls, profit sharing has been used as an effective tool to help promote teaming in a variety of settings. It works best in relatively small organizations (fewer than five hundred people) and requires regular and full disclosure of the unit's financial performance. Like gain sharing, profit sharing in itself doesn't make groups of people suddenly behave like teams, but it can serve to strengthen teams that already exist.

MERIT-BASED

Merit- or performance-based pay schemes all share one common characteristic: They are intended to reward employees for their individual contributions to the organization. Many question whether individual performance is relevant in team-based organizations and, therefore, if merit-based pay even has a place in a high performance team setting. The answer is yes, it can.

It is a fallacy to assume that individual performance is no longer important or relevant in team settings. In fact, in highly effective teams there are lots of stellar individual performers. Granted, there are numerous problems with the merit-based pay—it can, and many schemes do, emphasize individual performance at the expense of team development. But with some modification, it is possible to effectively reward individual performance without dismantling team effectiveness.

The key to using a merit-based approach in a team setting centers around three factors:

1. The criteria used to evaluate individual performance
2. The people chosen to evaluate individual performance
3. The extent to which the team is directly involved in defining the first two factors

The criteria used to evaluate individual performance in a team setting are very different from the criteria typically associated with performance-based pay schemes. Individual performance against standard or individual work-quality ratings is replaced with criteria that focus on individual contributions toward the development of team capability and performance. The new criteria include such things as:

- Ability to contribute ideas to the team
- Willingness to share job knowledge and skills with other team members
- Ability to problem-solve in a team setting
- Ability to make decisions in a team setting
- Resourcefulness and dependability
- Facilitation skills
- Ability to provide timely and accurate feedback to other team members
- Responsiveness to customer needs and desires
- Diversity of skills

In most cases the evaluator also changes. Generally, team members recognize their peers as having more direct and intimate knowledge of their job and their contributions than their manager has. This becomes particularly true with teams that are operating in an essentially self-regulating mode and have minimal management supervision. By using peer feedback or some combination of feedback from peers, management, and customers, team members can receive accurate evaluations of their performance.

While peer feedback can be a powerful tool for conveying accurate and constructive assessments, it can just as easily be used inappropriately and with destructive consequences. Many managers, not liking the difficulties associated with giving performance reviews, are only too glad to turn over this responsibility to the team. But turning over performance feedback to a team that has not been properly trained in good feedback techniques can prove disastrous. In one extreme instance, the individual being reviewed sat silently in the center of the room while her performance was openly discussed by other team members. In a round-table fashion, each team member described what he didn't like about the person being reviewed. Not only did the experience leave many participants angry or in tears, it proved to be highly divisive to the team. Much of the feedback had nothing to do with job performance or work behaviors. Some of the feedback even related to such irrelevant things as the person's choice of hairstyle!

Before peer feedback can be used effectively, several conditions need to be in place:

- All team members providing feedback must understand and be able to apply effective feedback techniques.
- The feedback must focus on those things the person does well and those areas where there are development opportunities.
- The feedback must focus on specific, observable behaviors and be nonjudgmental in nature.
- The team should make the decision as to whether they want to use peer feedback and if every team member's participation is required.
- Initially the feedback should be done anonymously (in a written format) and not tied to pay.
- The team must commit to reviewing the effectiveness of peer reviews and making continual improvements to the process.

In general, merit-based approaches work best if the team has direct input into the design of the system—particularly the key elements of what criteria will be used to evaluate individual performance and who will actually conduct the performance review. It is important that the criteria used to evaluate performance focus on how the individual is helping improve the effectiveness of the team.

SKILL-BASED

Pay for skills was originally developed as a means to promote cross-training and skill diversity. In achieving this goal, the approach—when effectively implemented—works fabulously.

The method is based on a simple formula: The more skills an employee can perform, the more money she receives. Those who can perform the most skills become the highest paid. The underlying assumption is that a multiskilled work force will enable the organization to be more flexible and efficient.

An advantage of the process is that it is relatively easy to administer—once an employee is certified at performing a skill, he receives a predetermined pay increase. There is none of the ambiguity, frustration, or bickering that often accompanies performance evaluations.

While the approach encourages skill acquisition, it does not necessarily reinforce other attributes—like problem solving, decision making, and interpersonal skills—that are important to the sustained performance of the team. Another potential negative is that the organization may be training and paying employees for acquiring a level of skill that's well beyond what's necessary to get the job done. Some organizations, recognizing this issue, put strict limitations on the number of people who can get cross-trained in the skill areas that carry the highest pay bonus. This creates another set of problems, foremost of which are employees who feel unfairly limited in trying to advance their skills and their pay.

Another criticism with pay for skills is that it can create "a jack of all trades, master of none" work force. Most programs guard against this potential liability by having skill certifications that require employees to demonstrate both the skill and a high level of proficiency in performing it. In some cases, skill recertifications are required on an annual basis to assure that the skill proficiency has been maintained.

Finally, pay for skills is ineffective (and inappropriate) in certain settings. It does not work well in professional teams where the amount of time to develop certain skills or areas of expertise is years or decades, not weeks or months. In these settings cross-training and skill diversity may not be cost effective or even necessary. One of the other reward methods will serve as a more effective incentive for such teams.

Despite these criticisms, pay for skills remains the vanguard method in many high performing teams—particularly in manufacturing settings. Its long-standing and proven record makes it a method worthy of serious consideration in settings where cross-training provides clear advantages to the organization's overall flexibility and responsiveness.

TACKLING THE PAY ISSUE

There are, of course, variations to these four basic compensation models. IBM Canada is using its existing merit-pay program to reward both individual and team performance. Each employee has a team taper (meaning a set of goals or objectives the team is attempting to achieve) and an individual taper that is focused on her personal objectives. Team members then determine what percentage of the performance rating is based on team versus individual performance. The percentages vary significantly among teams, but a clear tendency has emerged: The higher-performing, more cohesive teams tend to want a higher percentage of their overall review based on team, and not individual, performance.

Many organizations use a combination of approaches. Boeing's Corinth, Texas, plant, for example, uses a combination of skill- and merit-based pay. The secret to success has less to do with which approach (or combination of approaches) is utilized than it does with the timing of when the pay issue is addressed and the process that is followed in implementing the new reward system.

IMPLEMENTING THE NEW DESIGN

The following steps are helpful to consider when dealing with the pay issue. They provide a commonsense sequence and help clarify the role leaders and team members should play in the process.

1. Determine what is to be reinforced (leader driven).

Although compensation will be identified as a key issue by members of the work teams, the senior management of the organization should take an active role in sponsoring and facilitating the change effort. Early on, the sponsoring managers should develop a list that prioritizes the most critical behaviors that need to be reinforced for the continued development of the HPWS. The more clarity that can be developed regarding the types of behaviors to be reinforced, the easier it becomes in defining the components of the new reward package.

2. Develop a reward philosophy (leader driven).

The reward philosophy describes the fundamental belief the new system must be based upon. Examples of philosophy statements include:

- Pay is based on individual and team performance.
- The wealth that is created should be shared with all those who helped create it.
- Individual pay reflects the performance of the organization as a whole.
- Pay is based on the acquisition and application of new knowledge and skills.

There is no right or wrong reward philosophy. A philosophy that states that pay should be based on performance implies a merit or gain-sharing approach, while a philosophy stressing a sharing of wealth suggests a profit-sharing component—each could prove highly effective in reinforcing team performance. It is critical that the pay philosophy be widely understood within the organization before any work on the overall compensation system begins. In this way agreement and support on the intent of the new pay design can be gained early.

3. Determine boundary conditions (leader driven).

Virtually any project a team undertakes has certain constraints or limitations that must be considered, and developing a new pay system is certainly no exception. Some boundaries are obvious:

- The new system must not discriminate against any employee.
- It must fall within the current laws governing compensation practices.
- It must not raise payroll to an unacceptable level.

Other boundaries, also important, may need to be identified. Corporate compensation or union approval of the process, for example, may be necessary. The crucial point is that the sponsoring management team clearly define all the boundary conditions before any work on developing the new compensation package actually begins.

4. Form a design team and initiate the effort (leader/team driven).

Meaningful involvement will lead to commitment. It only makes sense that those directly affected by the new reward package should have a say in its design. This can be accomplished by forming a design team made up of a diagonal slice of the organization. The design team, working within the pay philosophy and boundary conditions outlined by the sponsoring managers, begins developing the new package.

5. Facilitate the development of the new design (leader/team driven).

Once the design team has begun its work, it is important for the sponsors to play an active role in supporting and facilitating their efforts. The design team may, for example, run into unforeseen issues from the corporate level or find they need additional time or extra resources to pull the new compensation package together. Wherever possible, the sponsoring managers should be in open communication with the design team and provide them ongoing support and encouragement.

6. Check the new design for consistency with the reinforcement list, pay philosophy, and boundary conditions (leader/team driven).

The acid test for the new design is threefold:

- It helps reinforce behaviors consistent with HPWTs.
- It is consistent with the pay philosophy.
- Its design does not violate any of the boundary conditions.

Together, the sponsoring managers and the design team should take a careful look at the proposed pay system and assess whether it meets these three criteria. If the design does not, then the specific concerns should be addressed in the next iteration of the package. If the design does meet all the criteria, then it's ready to be tested.

7. Try the new system (team driven).

Here the focus is in actually implementing the new system. It's very important that throughout their work the design team has been in open and direct communication with the employees they represent—when the new pay package is implemented it should not be met with shock or confusion.

8. Evaluate its effectiveness (team driven).

After seeing the new package in actual operation, its strengths and weaknesses will become readily apparent. Based on a full assessment of what worked well and what didn't, the design team develops a list of recommendations for specific improvements.

9. Implement improvements (team driven).

The design team implements the improvements prior to the next review. These final two steps (8 and 9) should be repeated after every review cycle so that the compensation system continually improves.

By altering the way pay is divvied out, people will not suddenly flock to teams and start operating as effective team members. Rather, pay is most effective as a means for strengthening teams that are already operational. For this reason, it is better for the reformer to lag changes to the pay system until later in the transition. The process outlined here helps in defining and developing a pay system that can reinforce and strengthen preexisting teams.

INSTITUTIONALIZING SUPPORT

The alignment of other support systems in conjunction with changing compensation plans (e.g., corporate staff, costing, site services, information systems) is equally important for the continued evolution of high performing teams. None, however, poses a bigger challenge to the reformer than the pay system—and hence the emphasis on it here. It is important to recognize, however, that the desired outcome of this stage of the implementation effort goes well beyond revamping the pay system. The real intent is to institutionalize support systems and practices that truly reinforce and strengthen the overall team-based design.

CHAPTER **12**

The Plateau Phenomenon

Just what does the future hold? Clearly, increasing numbers of managers—from settings as diverse as manufacturing, service, education, and government—are recognizing that speed, flexibility, and innovation are quickly replacing consistency, stability, and calculation as the desirable traits for organizations of the future. High performance management is not a periphery experiment any longer—it has become a commonly accepted, mainstream practice for improving competitiveness. In fact, the key to competitive advantage in the future may hinge on three factors: the *speed* with which high performance practices are implemented; the *size* of the organization they cover; and how *sustainable* they are within the organization over the long haul.

SUSTAINING A HIGH PERFORMANCE WORK SYSTEM

Sustainability is an important issue we have yet to discuss—especially in light of the fact that many transitions do not survive for more than a few years. Indeed, even some of the companies mentioned in this book have seen significant backtracking in their teaming efforts in recent years. Consider the following:

■ *Digital's Enfield, Connecticut, plant, once referred to as the "mecca of new organization design," was closed during a recent consolidation effort. Being one of the most publicized and well-documented examples of a HPWS in action—it was the star of a book and countless articles—DEC received more than fifteen hundred letters requesting that the plant be kept open from people all over the United States who had either toured or read about the facility when the shutdown was announced. Despite its continued stellar performance, the "greater good" of the corporation dictated its demise.*

■ *The Tektronix Portables Division first used HPWTs in its manufacturing department as the foundation for turning around a losing business. In one year, the division came from a $23 million loss to regaining profitability. In two years, it had become the most profitable division in the entire company. HPWTs were soon embraced and effectively applied in the division's engineering, marketing, finance, and human-resources departments. Many saw the division as one of the best examples of applying HPWSs broadly across an entire organization. Six years after the effort was initiated, leadership changes corresponded closely to a flattening of the division's performance. A decision to alter the company's structure by recentralizing resulted in the division's being completely disbanded two years later.*

■ *Martin Marietta's Space Launch Systems which, in a mere eighteen months, documented a savings of more than $10 million through its team efforts, saw its HPWTs begin to stumble when mandatory layoffs were announced. The downsizing was the result of significant defense cuts associated with the end of the Cold War and the limited commercial application of the organization's current technologies. While some teams continue to operate, the current instability has significantly reduced their effectiveness.*

In addition, organizations whose efforts are still relatively young leave many questions unanswered. Will IBM Canada be able to sustain its team development efforts with the continued restructuring going on within IBM U.S.? What effect will Emerson Electric's recent purchase of Fisher Controls have on the HPWTs in place there? Will Monsanto's recent downsizing have lingering effects on its showcase plants?

ANATOMY OF TEAMING IN COLLAPSE

The modern business world is a place of rapid, unprecedented change, and while HPWSs are far more adaptive and responsive than other methods of organizing, they are not—as the above examples show—infallible. Any organization can be overcome by pressures or sudden changes in business conditions that stretch it beyond its ability to cope, regardless of the management philosophy it employs.

When a team-based organization does collapse, it can often be attributed to one of two factors:

1. A lack of continued leadership sponsorship and support (the leadership void)
2. A restructuring which requires the consolidation of groups operating under dramatically different management philosophies (the cultural collision)

THE LEADERSHIP VOID

One of the great ironies of creating a more participative work culture is the degree to which the transition—particularly during the early stages of the effort—is leader dependent. It is equally significant that many of the organizations that have been able to effectively sustain HPWSs have seen a remarkable degree of continuity in leadership—commonly a decade or more!

This has some obvious implications. First, fast-track management rotations, where high-potential managers spend as little as one or two years leading an operation, can have a negative effect on the development of a HPWS. A more appropriate length of stay might be four or five years—a time period that allows the work culture to solidify.

Second, any time there is going to be a leadership change, candidates should be carefully screened before anyone is finally selected. A candidate's management philosophy, experience in leading team-based organizations, technical competence, and personal leadership style should be among the primary considerations. Further, the leadership transition should be carefully planned to create a minimal amount of disruption in the organization. It proves helpful, for example, if there is a one- to two-month overlap during which the incoming manager shadows the activities of the departing one. The teamwork they are able to display during this transition period can become a powerful symbol to the rest of the organization.

CULTURAL COLLISION

The last decade has seen an unprecedented amount of corporate restructuring. A recent Harvard study found that 70 percent of the managers surveyed from large firms (a thousand or more employees) had been through at least one major restructuring between 1989 and 1991.[1] Often the restructuring centers around the consolidation of similar processes and systems. The intent is to improve overall efficiency and cut costs by eliminating redundancy.

Typically, consolidation decisions are made without consideration of the culture of the groups that are being combined. Oversights of this magnitude can prove particularly negative to high performance teams, which will tend to view the consolidation as a demonstrated lack of commitment to the teaming philosophy on the part of management. Changes to the team's charter and membership—activities that typically accompany consolidations—will likely lead to a regression in the team's overall operating effectiveness.

Employees who have worked on a high performing team will often report that they "couldn't go back to the old way." The increased autonomy, the greater feeling of contribution, the ability to have a direct impact on decisions, the variety of skills they can perform, and the increased involvement in the business are all powerful sources of motivation. If these factors are removed—or perceived as being removed—by combining members with another, traditionally structured group, the result can be dismal. Many consolidation efforts have ended in failure, not because of technical or process-related problems, but due to a collision of very different work cultures and work experiences.

These tendencies can be mitigated if management makes it clear—and follows it through with concrete action—that the newly consolidated organization will operate as a HPWS. If a concerted and aggressive effort to develop a team-based work culture is not made, however, the group will inevitably fall into a traditional control pattern. HPWSs take more energy to create and to sustain than traditional forms of organizing groups. As a result, *the pathway of least resistance always flows against teaming*.

It's worth noting that in several instances where HPWS organizations faced the need for dramatic cost reductions, the teams took the lead in defining and executing the required actions—including defining a process for layoffs if other methods of cost cutting did not achieve certain goals. This again demonstrates the extraordinary effectiveness of teams—when truly treated like business partners—to deal with even the most difficult issues.

THE PLATEAU PHENOMENON

Either of these factors (the leadership void or the cultural collision) can lead to the demise of teams across an entire organization, division, or even company. In this sense they operate at a macro level, potentially affecting the sustainability of the entire HPWS. Another key factor affecting the longevity of the team system occurs at a more micro level—within the team itself.

Teams sometimes see a flattening of their individual performance. Though the time frame varies dramatically, some teams will reach a kind of plateau in as little as one or two years following the initial transition to the high performance team structure. When the plateau is hit, it is usually quite obvious—improvements have slowed, performance trends have flattened, problem solving lacks creativity and inspiration. By all outward appearances the team appears sluggish, even stagnant.

The reason for this tendency is simple: It is difficult to sustain the high levels of energy required for continual improvement over the long haul. At some point, a means to rejuvenate the team—in effect, to renew it—becomes necessary. The depletion of energy leading to the performance plateau can usually be traced to two seemingly contradictory sources that create the same outward-appearing phenomenon:

1. *Hyper-Criticality:* frustrations created by a commonly held perspective among team members that the team is not living up to its potential
2. *Invincibility:* an arrogance or sense of superiority that is perpetuated through the glorification of past accomplishments

HYPER-CRITICALITY

Often members of a team are the harshest critics of the team's performance. What might seem an extraordinary achievement to an outsider can become regarded within the team as a failure. While critically assessing past performance is a desirable trait, in excess it can be debilitating. One team member described it as "the pervasive blue funk." Focus becomes so oriented on "what went wrong" or "what could've been" that team members lose perspective on what they have been able to achieve. The accumulation of perceived failure ultimately manifests itself in a kind of *team burnout*.

This form of plateauing is analogous to the common experience weight lifters have when, after months of steady improvement, they find their performance stagnating or even in decline. In such circumstances, intensifying the workout schedule can actually break down muscle tissue and ultimately do more harm than good. What's needed is a rest period where the muscles can regenerate and ultimately strengthen. For teams, it is much the same—they, too, need periods of relaxation in order to sustain continuous improvement.

One of the most effective ways to snap hyper-criticality is to celebrate past accomplishments. This has three positive effects:

1. It helps the team appreciate how much they really have achieved.
2. It helps create a more relaxed and rejuvenated atmosphere.
3. It helps establish the team's current level of performance.

The celebration must be meaningful for the team and may or may not include some public display of their achievements. It is critical, however, for the team to alter its focus from "what is wrong" to "what is right." A formal celebration will often aid in this refocusing.

A second strategy for refocusing the team is to identify their performance relative to other comparable groups. The benchmarking will often help them recognize just how good their performance is relative to others. This will further help break the critical-thinking cycle.

INVINCIBILITY

While some teams take on the traits of hyper-criticality, others demonstrate a kind of *team arrogance*. Team members readily recognize their past achievements—often glorifying their significance. Again, this can be a powerful trait in moderation, but taken to extremes it can create complacency. Team members are so focused on their perceived superiority, they begin to lose perspective of how their relative performance may be slipping.

There are three ways to overcome this debilitating tendency. First, the team needs to know what their performance really is relative to comparable teams. Are they truly operating at a superior performance level or are their real capabilities actually less than those of comparable teams? The benchmarking process must be supported by, and the research actually conducted by, team members. The information they uncover can have a profound effect in focusing on performance improvement.

A second strategy is for the team to establish a breakthrough goal. The goal should be set at a level that the team generally agrees is "possible" but that, in order to be achieved, will require a substantial change in the team's current operating practices. Such a challenge will often create an initial burst of enthusiasm as team members examine pathways for achieving the goal.

Finally, it often proves helpful for the team to develop a vision of greatness that looks three to five years ahead. The visioning process helps change the focus from past accomplishments to what the future could hold. This process helps the team recommit to a new future.

ONGOING RENEWAL

It may seem ironic that after the energy and effort invested in implementing the HPWS, there will be a tendency for some teams to plateau. It's encouraging to remember that the resources needed for the rejuvenation of the team are contained within it. In fact, the more directly the renewal process involves the team, the more self-renewal capability the team develops.

Afterword

In the high-value enterprise, only one asset grows more valuable as it is used: the problem-solving, -identifying, and brokering skills of key people. Unlike machinery that gradually wears out, raw materials that become depleted, patents and copyrights that grow obsolete, and trademarks that lose their ability to comfort, the skills and insights that come from discovering new linkages between technologies and needs actually increase with practice.

From *The Work of Nations* by Robert B. Reich, 1991

When the Berlin Wall fell in 1989, commentators were quick to declare the event a "triumph for democracy" and a clear indication of the "superiority of free-market economics." The dramatic episode had an additional meaning journalists and politicians failed to recognize: It marked the end of the bureaucratic era. The inherent inefficiencies of "faceless" departments and bureaus, of autocratic decision making, of central planning and control, of rigid hierarchy and red tape had helped bring the wall tumbling down.

THE GENIUS OF THE PAST

For the first half of the century, bureaucracy was the genius of the age. It assured stability, hierarchy, specialization, and control. It was so superior to previous forms of organizing and managing, it represented the pinnacle of efficiency and management enlightenment. The most bureaucratic companies of this era were the ones to be emulated.

And yet we had many clues of bureaucracy's problem side. President Franklin Delano Roosevelt discovered early in his administration that newly formed departments and agencies were far more effective at enacting programs than existing ones. The new departments lacked the mountains of red tape and the endless levels of approval. There was a less formal chain of command, information flowed more freely, and those lower in the organization tended to have more autonomy and discretion in getting things done. But few took note of these clues—bureaucracy still reigned as king.

Today it has all changed. The breakup of the Soviet Union and the breakdown of IBM are symbols of the same message: The Bureaucratic Age is over.

THE GENIUS OF A NEW AGE

While the genius of our age has not yet been fully defined, we know many of its characteristics. Organizations of the twenty-first century will be smaller, more flexible, responsive, and innovative. Companies will strive to maintain and develop effective networks, alliances, and confederations much the way organizations of the past strove to create vertically integrated monoliths. People, the only truly appreciable asset found in an organization, will be seen as the key to competitive advantage—much the way size and technology were once viewed. At the centerpiece of this new era will be the HPWS.

We are on the cusp of the Age of Teaming. And while many remnants of classic management still cast their long shadows in countless organizations, the debate as to whether HPWSs are or are not effective has ended. The new debate centers around the transformation process itself: What is the most effective path for creating a HPWS?

CREATING A HIGH PERFORMING ORGANIZATION

The implementation approach I have described, and the accompanying commentary relating to the complexity of issues implementers will likely face, is an attempt at uncovering a natural pathway—a true *Transformation Pathway*—for creating high performing organizations. A HPWS represents a major shift in the very cultural fabric of the organization—its structures, processes, roles, responsibilities, and management systems all change in the new design. Without a clear route to follow, the odds of failure, as we have seen, are great.

The Transformation Pathway begins by establishing a champion who will initiate the effort (Leadership) and ends with the ongoing renewal of the work system (Renewal). The steps along the way—gaining the commitment of opinion leaders (Commitment), expanding the flow and access of information (Communication), forming teams and engaging them in work redesign (Redesign), and establishing support systems that reinforce the new design (Reinforcement)—build the foundation on which the new work culture will ultimately stand. These are the six phases for implementing a HPWS.

Numerous issues must be confronted in order to progress through each phase of the effort. Among the most critical are:

Leadership Phase

- Establishing a champion who will lead the effort
- Articulating a case for change and a vision of a possible future

Commitment Phase

- Addressing the doubts and uncertainties of middle managers
- Creating a climate that encourages risk taking and experimentation
- Developing a working blueprint that defines the type of teams and an overall implementation strategy

Communication Phase

- Moving from a "need to know" to "right to know" mode of information sharing
- Expanding training efforts to include a combination of technical, interpersonal, and business skills

Redesign Phase

- Assuring direct team involvement in the design and continual redesign of work systems and processes
- Utilizing the core principles of HPWSs in making work design trade-offs

Reinforcement Phase

- Establishing formal and informal rewards that reinforce teamwork
- Aligning support systems so they reinforce HPWSs

Renewal Phase

- Assuring that energy and effort are put toward the continual renewal and revitalization of the system

---

IN THE BALANCE

The challenges modern organizations face—whether in the industrial, service, government, or education sector—are without historical precedent. The life of many products is now measured in weeks or months, not years or decades; perfect quality is a customer expectation, not an expensive luxury; competition is worldwide, not domestic; citizens expect more from their government and education system while wanting less taxation—the list goes on and on. Becoming more efficient, effective, responsive, and flexible is no longer an option to be considered, it is a requirement that must be executed. Organization survival hangs in the balance. Recreating the workplace is, in these modern times, as necessary as it is inevitable.

Assessing Leadership Readiness

Given the importance of the role of champion to the transition to HPWSs, a relevant question becomes "Can it be taught?" Many managers have developed the necessary skills to take on this challenging position. A much larger pool has the potential but is not currently ready. The brief assessment that follows is intended to help potential champions identify their current strengths and weaknesses. Based on the results of the assessment, they can then create a personal development plan tailored to their specific needs.

Rate each of the following statements from 1 to 10 based on your assessment of how accurately it describes you.

KNOWLEDGE

1. I have lots of practical working experience in high performance organizations.

1	2	3	4	5	6	7	8	9	10

Highly inaccurate   *Highly accurate*

2. People say that I always demonstrate high performance practices in the way I manage my organization.

1	2	3	4	5	6	7	8	9	10

Highly inaccurate   *Highly accurate*

3. I am completely confident that I have all the right instincts to be an effective leader in a high performance workplace.

1	2	3	4	5	6	7	8	9	10

Highly inaccurate   *Highly accurate*

4. I have sufficient knowledge in the key concepts of high performance practices to begin a major change effort in the organization I manage.

1	2	3	4	5	6	7	8	9	10

Highly inaccurate   *Highly accurate*

5. I can describe in detail the risks as well as the benefits of implementing high performance management practices in my organization.

1	2	3	4	5	6	7	8	9	10

Highly inaccurate   *Highly accurate*

CONTACT

6. I regularly walk through the work area and talk to people.

1	2	3	4	5	6	7	8	9	10

Highly inaccurate   *Highly accurate*

7. People say I have my hand on the pulse of the organization—that I always know what's really going on.

1	2	3	4	5	6	7	8	9	10

Highly inaccurate   *Highly accurate*

8. People, at any level, regularly seek me out to discuss a variety of issues.

1	2	3	4	5	6	7	8	9	10

Highly inaccurate   *Highly accurate*

9. People feel comfortable talking with me; they say that I am a good listener.

1	2	3	4	5	6	7	8	9	10

Highly inaccurate   *Highly accurate*

10. People in the organization say they trust me and respect my opinion.

1	2	3	4	5	6	7	8	9	10

Highly inaccurate   *Highly accurate*

INFLUENCE

11. I have always been able to get the support I need for the proposals I have considered most important to my organization.

1	2	3	4	5	6	7	8	9	10

Highly inaccurate   *Highly accurate*

12. When people want to influence top-level managers, they ask me to help them.

1	2	3	4	5	6	7	8	9	10

Highly inaccurate   *Highly accurate*

13. My peers respect my judgment and abilities.

1	2	3	4	5	6	7	8	9	10

Highly inaccurate   *Highly accurate*

14. People say that I am an effective communicator and get my point across with ease.

1	2	3	4	5	6	7	8	9	10

Highly inaccurate   *Highly accurate*

15. The key managers in the organization respect my ideas and opinions and often act on my suggestions.

1	2	3	4	5	6	7	8	9	10

Highly inaccurate   *Highly accurate*

INTERPRETATION OF RESULTS AND UNDERLYING ASSUMPTIONS

Add up the ratings you gave in response to Items 1 to 5. This will give you an overall total score for the degree of *knowledge* you perceive you possess relating to high performance management practices. Do the same for Items 6 to 10 (this will give you an overall score that relates to the amount of *contact* you perceive you have with your organization) and Items 11 to 15 (this gives you an overall score that relates to how well you perceive your ability to *influence* peers and upper-level managers). These totals then relate to an overall readiness assessment scale (Figure 20), which attempts to define how ready you perceive yourself to lead the change effort among each of the three characteristics.

SCORE OF 38–50: READY

Scoring in this range for any of the three characteristics should be considered a confirmation of your perceived readiness. If, for example, you scored at this level in the characteristic *influence,* then you perceive yourself to have the necessary influencing capabilities to lead the change. Similarly, if you score in this range in all three characteristics, then you perceive yourself to be ready to champion the change effort.

It is important to remember that this assessment is based solely on how you perceive yourself. The perception that others in your organization have of your strengths and weaknesses is equally critical in

FIGURE 20: Readiness Assessment Scale

	Concentrated development required Total score 5 — 17	Opportunity Total score 18 — 37	Ready Total score 38 — 50
Knowledge			
Contact			
Influence			

undergoing the change and may be very different from your self-assessment. If you rated yourself in the *ready* range in any of the three categories, it is recommended that you solicit frank feedback from members within your organization to test your own self-perceptions. Do they see you as being ready? What kinds of additional development would they recommend?

SCORE OF 18–37: OPPORTUNITY

A score at this level signifies that as the potential champion, you probably need additional development before attempting to undergo the change effort. Depending on the characteristic that rates in the *opportunity* category, the development may take many different forms. Here are a few examples of possible development opportunities for each characteristic:

Knowledge: There are a variety of ways to gain access to information about HPWSs. The easiest method is to review the current literature on the subject. Many books have been written and a steady stream of articles is continually published in the major business and organization behavior journals.

A second source is conferences and workshops. Currently there is a variety of conferences, workshops, seminars, and networks available for individuals interested in heightening their understanding of these high performance concepts. These are a powerful way to be exposed to new ideas and meet a variety of people who are actually engaged in transforming organizations.

Finally, tours of facilities that have introduced HPWSs can be beneficial in understanding the real day-to-day mechanics of these kinds of work systems. Today there is a variety of plants that regularly offer tours representing virtually every industrial segment.

Contact: In the management classic *In Search of Excellence,* Tom Peters and Robert Waterman popularized the concept of "management by wandering around" (MBWA). The essence of this idea is that managers who are regularly seen in the work area are perceived as being less threatening and as genuinely concerned with the people in the organization. It is critical that managers spend time in the work area listening to people, talking with them, asking questions—in effect, getting their hands on the pulse of what is really going on.

From a development standpoint, this means actually scheduling large blocks of time to "wander around" the work area. Several general managers I have worked with regularly spend time working on the production line as a way to get better acquainted with members of the work force and to become more aware of the problems and frustrations they regularly face. Another way to gain more contact is through the location of your office. It is typical for managers in HPWSs to have their desks, without walls, near the center of the work area. Finally, the removal of unnecessary status barriers further helps in gaining contact. Neckties or suits, in many organizations, clearly delineate between managers and workers. Try going without a tie or wearing casual clothes. Eliminate other perks like special parking privileges or executive dining rooms.

Influence: The ability to effectively influence others as a way to gain both protection and support for the organization as it goes through the transition to HPWSs is a critical aspect of the leadership role. The first step in developing effective influencing abilities is in simply recognizing that it is a critical skill set to have. Too often managers believe that the inherent logic of an idea will gain widespread support for it. Organizations are essentially political in nature and often decisions are made based more on who the key supporters are than on rationale and logic.

In gaining support for high performance concepts, you must first have a clear *vision* of what it is you hope to achieve with the implementation of these concepts. This vision must have enough clarity that it will excite the imagination of others. A further feature of this vision is that it should show others, particularly upper-level managers, what they will gain by supporting this effort. The next element is to take advantage of *opportunities* to present this vision to other key individuals in the organization. Opportunities can be structured events, such as network meetings arranged for the express purpose of discussing high-involvement concepts, or "chance" occurrences like running into a key manager in the parking lot and discussing your vision with him or her. The final element in gaining influence is to behave with *tenacity*. Not everyone will agree with the vision of a possible future that has been developed. Some may even outwardly ridicule it. By being tenacious in your convictions and consistent in your actions, you continually strengthen your ability to influence others. The power of influence comes from the strength that others begin to see in your own personal commitment.

Effective influencing also requires respect, grace, and political savvy. Blaming others for the problems you encounter will do little more than alienate the very people whose support you will likely need for long-term success. When asking for their support, first demonstrate your recognition of their position and the issues they must contend with. When stating your own desires, focus on how the change you are seeking will benefit not just your team, but the company as a whole. Once you've established the benefits of the change, be very clear about how they can best help you.

SCORE OF 5–17: CONCENTRATED DEVELOPMENT REQUIRED

A score at this level suggests that a significant commitment to personal development should be undertaken before you attempt to lead the effort to implement high performance work systems. The personal development program you go through should include many of the features just outlined in the opportunity category. In contemplating what this score means to you personally, the following questions should be considered:

- *Is it possible that your perception of your abilities is unusually harsh? Would others in the organization tend to see you as more effective than you are likely to see yourself?*
- *Is it possible that you are not the right person to lead this change? If you are not the right person, then who is?*

APPENDIX **B**

The Implementation Checklist

A basic assumption of the Transformation Pathway is that early phases build the foundation for later ones. Phase I, for instance, will *usually* need to be established before Phase II can effectively begin. While no change effort will follow a completely sequential or linear path—organizations are far too complex and unpredictable for that—this model can be valuable in helping (1) maintain a consistent focus on the overall direction of the change and (2) evaluate progress. By using this checklist, change agents will be able to assess the current state of the implementation effort and be in a good position to determine the necessary next steps to assure that the transition follows a smooth path.

For each of the statements that follow, respond either "yes" or "no." A "yes" response means you believe the actions, behaviors, structures, systems, roles, and/or processes depicted in the statement are in place in the organization you are assessing. A "no" response means that you believe they are not in place.

Is the statement accurate? (Check one circle for each statement.)

Yes   No

PHASE I: LEADERSHIP

1. There is a clearly identifiable individual(s) who has the necessary knowledge of employee empowerment, influence within the organization's hierarchy, and contact with the day-to-day "workplace" realities to serve as the champion to the change effort. This individual(s) has shown a strong desire to champion the effort as demonstrated by a willingness to dedicate budget, resources, and personal time.   ◯   ◯

2. The "case for change" that provides the business rationale for significantly improving the organization's overall performance has been clearly defined and communicated with formal and informal leaders within the organization.   ◯   ◯

3. An organization profile has been developed that links overall business strategy and direction with a possible future. This scenario serves as the model or vision of what the organization is capable of achieving. This vision has been widely shared with formal and informal leaders within the organization.   ◯   ◯

4. A systematic plan has been developed that describes the sequence of change to the organization's systems, processes, and structures.   ◯   ◯

	Yes	*No*

PHASE II: COMMITMENT

5. The leadership team that will coordinate the change effort has been identified (including key "formal" and "informal" leaders within the organization whose support for a successful effort will be critical). ○ ○

6. The leadership of the organization has been given a realistic preview of what will be required of them during the change effort. This preview includes such things as visits to selected facilities, conversations with experienced change agents, readings/study sessions, and attendance at selected conferences/seminars. ○ ○

7. The case for change, organization profile, vision and transition plan are clearly understood and supported by the members of the leadership team. This team has had opportunities to influence and upgrade the work originated by the champion of the change effort. ○ ○

8. The leadership team has developed and committed to a process for communicating the case for change, vision of the future, and the transition strategy to the rest of organization. ○ ○

9. The leadership team is highly visible during the initial communication of the organization/culture change effort. ○ ○

10. There are few "status" distinctions between managers and workers. Management perks

Yes *No*

are minimal. There is a clear intention to minimize artificial barriers that would be detrimental to creating an open, highly participative work environment. This trend toward lessening and/or eliminating these distinctions is strongly supported by the leadership team. ○ ○

PHASE III: COMMUNICATION

11. Information-sharing processes such as "team meetings" and "state-of-the-business" assemblies are a regular part of the work week. In these sessions, people throughout the organization have direct access to the original source of the data. ○ ○

12. The case for change, organization profile, and transition plan have been openly communicated to all employees within the organization. ○ ○

13. All managers, supervisors, technical and support professionals, and team members have been formally introduced to the concepts of high performance work teams through an educational experience. ○ ○

14. A process is in place, including training and follow-up support, to help supervisors, managers, and technical and support professionals expand their roles to include (1) becoming a living example and role model for others (*Living Example*), (2) having the ability to coach others and develop their poten-

Yes   *No*

tial (*Coach*), (3) being able to see changes in the business environment and translate those changes into specific responses that benefit the organization (*Business Analyzer*), (4) demonstrating a willingness to run interference for the team and bust through barriers that are unduly constraining improvement opportunities (*Barrier Buster*), (5) bringing together the necessary resources that enable team members to carry out their innovative ideas (*Facilitator*), (6) serving as a customer advocate by keeping the team focused on the desires, interests, and needs of the customer (*Customer Advocate*), and (7) being an effective leader who unleashes energy and enthusiasm by creating a vision that others find inspiring and motivating (*Leader*).   ◯   ◯

15. Clearly identifiable teams are utilized (as opposed to individual job functions or independent work stations) as the primary unit for organizing the work area. Each of these teams has a clearly developed charter or mission, as well as operating guidelines, and meets on a regular basis to address issues, problems, and ways to improve overall operating effectiveness.   ◯   ◯

16. The information flow is adequate and timely. People at all levels understand the current performance of the business (e.g., customers, competition, strategies, profitability) and ef-

Yes   *No*

fectively utilize operational data (e.g., quality, service level, schedule, etc.) for problem identification, resolution, and improvement recommendations. ○   ○

17. Appropriate education programs are designed and implemented to allow closer and more effective working relationships with suppliers and customers. These relationships are further augmented by the open and continuous flow of relevant information. Mangement regularly provides customer/supplier feedback and sets up opportunities for direct, face-to-face meetings between team members and customers/suppliers. These communication linkages are regularly used to identify process and product improvements. ○   ○

PHASE IV: REDESIGN

18. A structured method to examine work flow and processes is conducted by work teams to improve the effectiveness of the operation. This structured method includes an assessment of the current environment facing the organization, an assessment of the technical requirements needed to perform the work, and an assessment of the skills/areas of knowledge and corresponding work structure needed to support the work. Work flow and processes are continually redesigned and improved by these work teams. ○   ○

19. A process is in place, including training and follow-up support, to help team members

	Yes	*No*

expand their roles to include (1) having a strong awareness of the customer's wants and needs coupled with opportunities to meet them (*Customer Advocate*), (2) showing a willingness to train and develop others by sharing knowledge and skills (*Trainer*), (3) continually expanding personal knowledge and applying it to the workplace (*Resource*), (4) demonstrating the necessary technical skills to perform the job effectively (*Skilled Worker*), (5) working and communicating well with other team members and business associates (*Team Player*), (6) being able to assimilate and utilize information for making decisions that directly impact the team (*Decision Maker*), and (7) identifying and addressing problems that occur in the work area (*Problem Solver*).   ○   ○

20. There is a formalized skill-development process in place (e.g., rotation through different job areas) that allows people to learn a variety of usable skills.   ○   ○

21. Team members have the freedom to take direct action whenever they encounter a problem that is likely to impact quality, cost, schedule, and/or output.   ○   ○

22. Work teams are directly involved in establishing quantitative and qualitative measurements to track the operational effectiveness of the group. This information provides feedback to the teams about their overall performance.   ○   ○

	Yes	*No*

23. Everyone in the organization can state who their key customers, key competitors, and key suppliers are. They can also describe what differentiates the product/service they build/support from others in the marketplace. People will further state that they apply this knowledge in making decisions that affect their work area.   ◯   ◯

PHASE V: REINFORCEMENT

24. Openness, honesty, and constructive feedback are highly valued and demonstrated organizational traits. Manager and peer feedback occur on a routine basis. Managers also receive regular feedback from the people they manage.   ◯   ◯

25. The work teams, and the functions they perform, are almost entirely self-contained and managed by the group itself. Group members rely on one another for cross-training, problem solving, the handling of administrative duties, and mutual support.   ◯   ◯

26. There is a high concentration of "generalists" who have a wide breadth and deep scope of skills. Functions or jobs that require high levels of specialization are closely associated with the work teams that their specialty supports.   ◯   ◯

27. Thorough employment planning is in place to help reduce the negative effects of rapid

	Yes	*No*
changes in product/service demand and/or profitability.	○	○

28. There is an overall reward and pay strategy in place that uses a variety of methods and sources to recognize, reward, and reinforce appropriate behaviors and results. ○ ○

29. People are rewarded based on the skills and the work-related knowledge they possess and on their ability to apply them to the improvement of the business. The number of jobs/skills individuals perform is continually expanding. This expansion has increased flexibility and autonomy and lessens the need for narrowly defined, fractionated jobs. Correspondingly, job descriptions are broader in their focus and content. ○ ○

PHASE VI: RENEWAL

30. All members of the organization can describe the major achievements of the change effort. These achievements are formally celebrated. ○ ○

31. The critical learnings from the change effort have been formally documented and are being integrated into future organization development plans. ○ ○

32. The case for change has been updated to reflect new business realities. These include changes in customers/markets, technology, competition, environment, politics/government, demographics, suppliers, and economics. ○ ○

	Yes	*No*

33. The organization profile and vision of the future have been updated by the leadership team to describe the next level of possible achievement. ◯ ◯

INTERPRETING RESULTS

As the organization progresses through one phase, it has created a foundation on which the next phase of the change effort can stand. An organization would be best prepared to begin Phase IV activities, for example, *only after* it has successfully progressed through Phases I, II, and III. Conversely, it would rarely make sense to begin re-designing work (a Phase IV activity) if it is unlikely that management will support the changes that are identified (a Phase I and II activity). In this example, the work redesign would be built on an unstable foundation since there would be a general lack of management support for the newly created redesign.

To determine which phase the organization you assessed is in, look over your responses. For progression through a phase to be complete, all the statements related to that phase and all statements related to any earlier phases must be answered in the affirmative ("yes"). As an example, for progression through Phase III to be complete, Statements 1 to 18 would all have to be rated "yes."

Notes

CHAPTER 1: THE AGE OF TEAMING

1. Martin, Tim. "Levi Launches Team Manufacturing," *The Seattle Times/Seattle Post-Intelligencer,* December 13, 1992.
2. Sheridan, John H. "Frank Merlotti: A Master of Empowerment," *Industry Week,* January 7, 1991, p. 26.
3. Schilder, Jana. "Work Teams Boost Productivity," *Personnel Journal,* February 1992, p. 68.
4. Stewart, Thomas A. "The Search for the Organization of Tomorrow," *Fortune,* May 18, 1992, p. 93.
5. Ibid., p. 94.

CHAPTER 2: THE ENDURING LEGACY

1. Babbage, Charles. *On the Economy of Machinery and Manufacturers.* London: Charles Knight, 1832.
2. Toffler, Alvin. *The Third Wave.* New York: William Morrow and Company, 1981, p. 40.
3. Taylor, Frederick W. *The Principles of Scientific Management.* New York: Harper, 1911, p. 64.
4. Ibid., p. 36.
5. Toffler, op. cit., pp. 42–43.
6. Gilberth, Frank B. *Primer of Scientific Management.* New York: Van Nostrand, 1914, p. 50.
7. Taylor, op. cit., p. 43.
8. Ibid., pp. 72–73.

9. Taylor, James C. "Job Design Criteria Twenty Years Late." In *Design of Jobs* 2nd edition, edited by Louis E. Davis and James C. Taylor. Santa Monica, Calif.: Goodyear Publishing, 1979, pp. 56–57.

10. Lincoln, James R. "Employee Work Attitudes and Management Practices in U.S. and Japan: Evidence from a Large Comparative Study," *California Management Review*, Fall 1989, p. 95.

11. I first encountered the idea of a "control paradigm" from Marvin Weisbord. See Weisbord, Marvin R. *Productive Workplaces: Organizing and Managing for Dignity, Meaning and Community*. San Francisco: Jossey-Bass, 1987, p. 170.

12. Roach, Stephen S. "Services Under Siege—The Restructuring Imperative," *Harvard Business Review*, September–October 1991, pp. 82–91.

13. Ingrassia, Paul, and Joseph B. White. "Losing the Race: With Its Market Share Sliding, GM Scrambles to Avoid a Calamity," *Wall Street Journal*, December 14, 1989.

14. Tetzeli, Rick. "Making Quality More Than a Fad," *Fortune*, May 18, 1992, p. 12.

15. Schlesinger, Leonard A., and James L. Heskett "The Service-Driven Company," *Harvard Business Review*, September–October 1991, p. 74.

16. Ibid., p. 76.

17. McCall, Tom, with Steve Neal. *Tom McCall: Maverick*. Portland, Ore.: Binford and Mort, 1977, pp. 110–111.

18. Stewart, Thomas A. "The Search for the Organization of Tomorrow," *Fortune*, May 18, 1992, p. 95.

CHAPTER 3: THE TRANSFORMATION PATHWAY

1. Portions of the Kodak case first appeared in an article I co-authored with Kim Fisher for the work in America Institute. It was titled "Creating a High Performance Management Team: Eastman Kodak's 13 Room" and appeared in *The Manager as Trainer, Coach and Leader: Part 3*, edited by Jerome M. Roscow and Robert Zager, 1991. (Used with permission of the publisher.)

2. The cartoon appears in Gary Larson's book *It Came From the Far Side*. Kansas City, Mo.: Andrew and McMeel, 1986, p. 51.

3. There are circumstances—albeit rare—when pay must be addressed early in the transition. These instances are described in Chapter 11.

CHAPTER 4: THE MAKING OF A CHAMPION

1. Etherington, Bill. "The Challenge of Change," *IBM Insight,* February 1992, p. 1.

2. Sheridan, John H. "Frank Merlotti: A Master of Empowerment," *Industry Week,* January 7, 1991, p. 26.

3. An abbreviated version of this case first appeared in an article I co-authored with Janice Klein entitled "Managing Knowledge Worker Involvement: Three Managers' Stories," in *The Manager as Trainer, Coach and Leader: Part 1,* edited by Jerome M. Roscow and Robert Zager, the Work in America Institute, 1988 (used with permission from the publisher). While all events described in this story are true, the names John Preston and Z-Tech are pseudonyms.

CHAPTER 5: THE ESSENTIALS OF MAJOR CHANGE

1. Stayer, Ralph. "How I learned to Let My Workers Lead," *Harvard Business Review,* November–December, 1990, p. 9.

2. Beer, Michael, Russell A. Eisenstat, and Bert Spector. "Why Change Programs Don't Produce Change," *Harvard Business Review,* November–December, 1990, p. 159.

3. Ibid., p. 159.

4. Sheridan, John H. "Frank Merlotti: A Master of Empowerment," *Industry Week,* January 7, 1991, p. 27.

CHAPTER 6: DESPERATELY SEEKING EMPOWERMENT

1. Fisher, Anne B. "Morale Crisis," *Fortune,* November 18, 1991, p. 70.

2. I first explored the role of the change influencer in an article I co-authored with William Belgard and Kim Fisher titled "Vision, Opportunity, and Tenacity: Three Informal Processes That Influence Formal Transformation" in *Corporate Transformation: Revitalizing Organizations for a Competitive World,* edited by Ralph A. Kilmann and Teresa Joyce Covin, San Francisco: Jossey-Bass, 1988. I have borrowed con-

cepts from the original work and several passages. (Used with permission from the publisher.)

CHAPTER 7: THE DILEMMA IN THE MIDDLE

1. Fisher, Anne B. "Morale Crisis," *Fortune,* November 18, 1991, p. 71.
2. Robinson, Ron M., Sharon L. Oswald, Kerry S. Swinehart, and Jeffery Thomas. "Southwest Industries: Creating High-Performance Teams for High-Technology Production," *Planning Review,* November–December 1991, p. 11.
3. Verespej, Michael A. "When You Put the Team in Charge," *Industry Week,* December 3, 1990, p. 32.
4. Fisher, op. cit., pp. 71–72.
5. Robinson et al., op. cit., p. 11.
6. Kirkpatrick, David. "Breaking Up IBM," *Fortune,* July 27, 1992, p. 53.
7. Ibid., p. 53.
8. Hoerr, John. "The Cultural Revolution at A.O. Smith," *Business Week,* May 29, 1989, p. 68.
9. Sheridan, John H. "Frank Merlotti: A Master of Empowerment," *Industry Week,* January 7, 1991, p. 27.

CHAPTER 9: THE INFORMATION TRANSFER

1. Soloman, Charlene Marwer. "Behind the Wheel at Saturn," *Personnel Journal,* June 1991, p. 73.

CHAPTER 10: THE NEW AGENTS OF DESIGN

1. Weisbord, Marvin. "Participative Work Design: A Personal Odyssey," *Organizational Dynamics,* 1984, p. 18.
2. Ellis, James E. "Why Monsanto Is Plunking Down Its Chips on R&R," *Business Week,* August 21, 1987, p. 67.
3. Templin, Neal. "Team Spirit: A Decisive Response to Crisis Brought Ford Enhanced Productivity," *Wall Street Journal,* December 15, 1992.
4. Larson, Clint. "Team Tactics Can Cut Product Development Costs," *Journal of Business Strategy,* September–October 1988, p. 22.

5. Versteeg, Anna. "Self-Directed Work Teams Yield Long-Term Benefits," *Journal of Business Strategy,* November–December 1990, p. 9.

6. Guest, Robert H. "Team Management Under Stress," *Across the Board,* May 1989, p. 31.

7. These seven principles are based on the work of Albert Cherns. See "The Principles of Sociotechnical Design," *Human Relations,* 1976, vol. 29, pp. 783–92.

CHAPTER 11: THE REINFORCEMENT FACTOR

1. Feinstein, Selwyn. "Pay Satisfaction," *Wall Street Journal,* October 10, 1990.

2. Gellene, Denise. "Companies Reconsider Their Sales Incentives," *The Oregonian,* July 12, 1992.

3. Santora, Joyce. "Du Pont Returns to the Drawing Board," *Personnel Journal,* February 1991, pp. 34–36.

4. Ost, Edward J. "Team-Based Pay: New-Wave Strategic Incentives," *Sloan Management Review,* Spring 1990, pp. 19–27.

CHAPTER 12: THE PLATEAU PHENOMENON

1. Kanter, Rosabeth Moss. "Transcending Business Boundaries: 12,000 World Managers View Change," *Harvard Business Review,* May–June 1991, p. 159.

Index

About the Author

Steven R. Rayner has emerged as a leading authority on high per-forming organizations. He is cofounder of Belgard•Fisher•Rayner, Inc., a high performance work system training and consulting firm.

Rayner is author of numerous articles on the subject of high performance work systems, including those published by the Work in America Institute, the American Society for Training and Devel-opment, Oregon State University, the University of Minnesota, and Jossey-Bass Publishers. In addition, he has written articles for inter-nal publication for several major corporations, including Tektronix and Monsanto.

Rayner regularly speaks at industry, academic, and professional conferences on the subject of high performance work systems. He has addressed audiences at the Ecology of Work and Canadian Ecol-ogy of Work conferences, the Association of Quality and Participa-tion Conference, the American Production and Inventory Control Society, and the International Conference on Self-Managed Work Teams, as well as company- and academic-sponsored conferences including those hosted by the University of Pittsburgh, the Univer-sity of North Texas, Oregon State University, Digital Equipment Corporation, Esso Resources, Tektronix, and Texas Instruments.

Rayner's firm has worked with a number of companies in imple-menting high-involvement practices across North America and Western Europe. Its clients include Apple Computer, Corning, Fisher Controls, Goodyear, IBM, Martin Marietta, Monsanto, Rockwell, Shell Oil, and Weyerhaeuser.